First published by © Bonnier Fakta 2019
The English language edition published in 2020 by Hardie Grant
Books, an imprint of Hardie Grant Publishing

Hardie Grant Books (London)
5th & 6th Floors
52–54 Southwark Street
London SE1 1UN

Hardie Grant Books (Melbourne)
Building 1, 658 Church Street
Richmond, Victoria 3121

hardiegrantbooks.com

British Library Cataloguing-in-Publication Data. A catalogue record
for this book is available from the British Library.

Fire, Smoke, Green

ISBN 978-78488-326-3

Text © Martin Nordin
Food Photography © Martin Nordin
Portraits and other photography © Oskar Falck
Graphic design and illustrations: Katy Kimbell and Li Söderberg
Editor: Thomas Lundvall

For the English hardback edition:
Publishing Director: Kate Pollard
Editor: Eila Purvis
Translator: Ian Giles
Copy-editor: Lisa Pendreigh

Colour Reproduction by p2d
Printed and bound in China by Leo Paper Products Ltd.

FIRE

SMOKE

GREEN

MARTIN NORDIN

**VEGETARIAN BARBECUE, SMOKING
AND GRILLING RECIPES**

Hardie Grant

BOOKS

#1 BARBECUE STRAIGHT ON THE GRILL

GRILLED CAULIFLOWER with gremolata

Serves 6

2 cauliflower heads
100 ml (3½ fl oz/scant ½ cup) rapeseed
   (canola) oil
150 g (5 oz/⅔ cup) unsalted butter
salt

Gremolata
6 tablespoons finely chopped parsley leaves
2 tablespoons pine nuts, toasted
1 tablespoon finely chopped green chilli
1 tablespoon finely chopped garlic
1 unwaxed lemon, finely zested
sea salt flakes

To serve
90 g (3½ oz) whitecurrants

1 Light the barbecue (grill) and let the charcoal take on a strong, even glow. Prepare a package to cook the cauliflower in by putting a slightly smaller sheet of baking parchment on top of a slightly larger sheet of kitchen foil. Keep close to hand.

2 Mix all the ingredients for the gremolata in a bowl.

3 Slice each cauliflower head into three 'steaks'. Cut from the root end so that you have a piece of root attached to each slice. Lightly brush both sides of each slice with oil.

4 Grill the pieces of cauliflower so that they take on some grill marks. Place them on the baking parchment, cover with the butter and season with salt. Fold the package together to create a sealed parcel and place it back on the barbecue – preferably in a position that is less hot – and close the lid.

5 Open the package after about 30 minutes and check that the cauliflower has turned a beautiful shade of golden-brown and is starting to soften. The florets should flex if you press them gently. Take the temperature of the root – when it is around 80°C (180°F), the cauliflower is ready.

6 Place one slice of cauliflower on each plate, dollop a large tablespoon of gremolata onto each slice and top with the whitecurrants.

BOOST THE FLAVOUR **Use the parsley stalks in the gremolata – chop them as small as you can. This delivers a delicious, deep, slightly bitter parsley flavour, which compliments the other flavours in this dish nicely.**

GRILLED CORN with creamy pecorino sauce

Serves 6

6 corn cobs in their husks

150 g (5 oz/⅔ cup) unsalted butter at
    room temperature

2 garlic cloves, finely chopped

sea salt flakes

Lemon oil

shaved peel of ½ unwaxed lemon

100 ml (3½ fl oz/scant ½ cup) rapeseed
    (canola) oil

Pecorino sauce

2 shallots, finely chopped

2 tablespoons unsalted butter

1 tablespoon white wine vinegar

200 ml (7 fl oz/scant 1 cup) whipped cream

200 g (7 oz) grated (shredded) pecorino
    or alternative hard sheep's cheese

To serve

Fermented Tree Onions or garlic cloves, see recipe
    on p. 174

1 Bring a large saucepan of lightly salted water to the boil.

2 Fold down the leaves on the corn and remove any threads between the leaves and corn. Place the cobs in the water with the tip facing down and boil for around 5 minutes. Remove the corn from the pan and fold the leaves back around the cobs.

3 Mix the butter and garlic in a bowl using a fork. Set aside.

4 Heat the lemon peel and oil in a small saucepan. Remove the pan from the heat when it starts to simmer and leave to stand for around 10 minutes so that the oil takes on the flavour of the lemon. Remove the lemon skin from the oil and set aside.

5 Fry the shallots in butter on a low heat so that they soften but do not start to brown then add the vinegar. Continue stirring until the shallots have absorbed the vinegar. Mix in the cream and cook for another 3 minutes. Using a hand-held blender or food processor, blend the sauce until smooth and stir in the grated cheese. Season with salt.

6 Light the barbecue (grill). Place the corn on the barbecue while the charcoal is still burning. If you prefer, you can put them straight onto the burning charcoal. Grill the corn until the leaves are almost completely black – they act as a protective cover on the corn.

7 Remove the corn from the barbecue, fold down the leaves and spread the corn with the garlic butter.

8 Spoon a little of the sauce onto a plate and place a cob on top. Drizzle with lemon oil and top with some chopped Fermented Tree Onions or garlic cloves.

GRILLED PEAS AND SPRING ONIONS
with mint and bean sprouts

Serves 6

12 small spring onions (scallions)

3 tablespoons olive oil

1 kg (2 lb 4 oz) peas in pods

125 g (4 oz) bean sprouts

10 g (½ oz) chopped mint leaves

sea salt flakes

1 Light the barbecue (grill) and let the charcoal take on a soft glow.

2 Split the spring onions lengthways – try to keep some of the leaves. Brush the cut edges of the onions with oil. Place the spring onions on the barbecue and leave them until they have taken on some colour and started to soften – this should take around 10 minutes. Turn them over and grill on the other side for around 5 minutes. Place the spring onions in a large bowl and set aside.

3 Place the peas in their pods on the barbecue and leave them until the pods start to blacken – this should take around 5 minutes. Turn them over and leave for a further 5 minutes. Remove from the barbecue and allow them to cool. When the pods are cool enough to handle remove the peas from the pods and place the peas in the bowl with the spring onions.

4 Drizzle the remainder of the oil into the bowl, then add the bean sprouts and mint. Stir so that everything is airy, ideally using your hands, and season with salt. Place onto a large plate and serve as a side dish or a starter.

SHIITAKE MUSHROOMS with whisky and miso-marinade

Serves 6

600 g (1 lb 5 oz) shiitake mushrooms

Whisky and miso marinade

4 tablespoons whisky, preferably Balvenie or
     another Speyside or Japanese whisky

4 tablespoons rapeseed (canola) oil

2 tablespoons dark miso

2 tablespoons tamari

juice of ½ lime

1 tablespoon cane sugar

1 garlic clove

1 teaspoon sesame oil

To serve

6 egg yolks

1 tablespoon thyme leaves

sea salt flakes

cornflower petals (optional)

<u>1</u> Mix together all the ingredients for the marinade using a hand-held blender or food processor.

<u>2</u> Clean the mushrooms and cut into slices 3–4 mm (⅛ in) thick. Place them on a sheet of baking parchment and brush with the marinade. Turn them over and brush the other side.

<u>3</u> Light the charcoal in the barbecue (grill) and let it take on a fine, soft glow. Grill the mushrooms on the barbecue, turning them over occasionally and brushing them with a little more marinade. Once the mushrooms take on a nice, caramelised golden-brown colour, they are done.

<u>4</u> Plate up the mushrooms. Place an egg yolk in the middle of the plate and top with thyme, sea salt flakes and some cornflower petals, if you have some to hand.

BEER-MARINATED AUBERGINE with tomato sauce and shiitake mushrooms tossed in butter

Serves 6

Beer-marinated aubergine

3 large aubergines (eggplants)

330 ml (11¼ fl oz/1⅓ cups) beer, e.g. brown ale

2 garlic cloves, lightly crushed

2 tablespoons malt vinegar

2 teaspoons salt

Tomato sauce

6 large tomatoes

2 tablespoons olive oil

2 small yellow onions, finely chopped

1 tablespoon tomato purée (paste)

1 tablespoon white wine vinegar

1 tablespoon powdered sea buckthorn

100 ml (3½ fl oz/scant ½ cup) mushroom stock

salt (optional)

Shiitake mushrooms tossed in butter

2 tablespoons rapeseed (canola) oil

300 g (10½ oz) shiitake mushrooms

2 tablespoons unsalted butter

1 tablespoon whisky, preferably Balvenie from
    Speyside (optional)

salt

To serve

2–3 sprigs of coriander (cilantro)

1 Cut the aubergine into slices 1–1½ cm (½ in) thick. Mix the rest of the ingredients for the marinade together in a plastic bag then add the slices of aubergine. Rub the aubergine through the bag so that the marinade is evenly distributed. Leave to rest in the refrigerator for 7–8 hours. Take it out a few times and rub the aubergine or shake the bag to ensure the aubergine is evenly coated in the marinade.

2 Halve the tomatoes then coarsely grate them into a bowl. Once you have finished grating, you should only have the tomato skin left in your hand.

3 Add the olive oil to a frying pan (skillet) on a medium heat and gently brown the onions. Add the tomato purée and raise the temperature slightly. Stir with a wooden spoon for around 5 minutes so that the tomato purée takes on a more intense, darker colour. Add the vinegar, powdered sea buckthorn, mushroom stock and the grated tomatoes. Reduce the heat, add salt to taste, if required, and leave to simmer for 20–30 minutes. Strain the tomato sauce so that it is smooth – I usually use a sieve (fine-mesh strainer).

4 Light the charcoal in the barbecue (grill) and let it take on a steady, fine glow. Take the aubergine slices out of the marinade. Place them on paper towels and blot the cut edges until dry. Grill the aubergine slices until they turn a deep colour and have a crust.

5 Heat the rapeseed oil in a frying pan and wait until it is smoking. Add the mushrooms and fry them until they begin to colour. Lower the heat slightly and add the butter. Stir to ensure that the mushrooms are covered in the butter, and season with salt. I usually add some whisky when frying mushrooms, so add a tablespoon or so if you have any. Continue frying for a few more minutes and then set the mushrooms aside.

6 Serve either on a plate or in a bowl. Pour out a little tomato sauce, place the aubergine slices in the sauce and top with the mushrooms and coriander.

GRILLED ASPARAGUS with burrata, egg yolk and kumquat sauce

Serves 6

1 kg (2 lb 4 oz) asparagus

2 tablespoons rapeseed (canola) oil

Kumquat sauce

12 kumquats, sliced

2 tablespoons grated fresh turmeric

1 vanilla pod (bean), split lengthways

3 star anise

100 ml (3½ fl oz/scant ½ cup) honey

300 ml (10 fl oz/1¼ cups) water

To serve

6 burrata balls

6 egg yolks

6 tablespoons Roasted Buckwheat, see recipe on
   p.170

chive flowers (or another onion flower)

6 teaspoons Leek Ash, see recipe on p. 67

1 Light the barbecue (grill) and let the charcoal take on a fine glow.

2 Make the kumquat sauce. Bring all the ingredients to the boil in a saucepan on a high heat. Boil for around 10 minutes until it begins to thicken and is foaming a lot. Strain the sauce into a bowl through a sieve (fine-mesh strainer) and press as much of the kumquat fruit through as possible.

3 Trim and wash the asparagus. Ideally, peel them all the way to the top – you don't have to, but it looks good! Dry them and place in a bowl together with the rapeseed oil. Mix so that they are covered in the oil then place the asparagus on the barbecue. Roll them back and forth constantly for around 5 minutes, taking care to ensure they don't burn too much. Remove them from the grill once they have blacked slightly.

4 Take a burrata ball and tear it in half using your hands. Place it on a plate and let the cream drain out. Place a pile of asparagus beside it, put an egg yolk on the burrata and cut into it so that the yolk runs out. Drizzle with 3–4 tablespoons of kumquat sauce. Top with Roasted Buckwheat, chive flowers and Leek Ash.

GRILL THE STALKS **The stalks of chive flowers and onion flowers are almost inedible when raw – they're hard and wooden. But if you grill them, they're great to eat and offer a lovely onion tone.**

MEZCAL with grilled grapefruit

6 drinks

6 ruby grapefruit (about 600 ml/20 fl oz/2½ cups)
    juice after grilling and pressing)
12 tablespoons cane sugar
60 ml (2 fl oz/¼ cup) beetroot (beet) juice
360 ml (12 fl oz/1½ cups) mezcal (or a smoky
    tequila)
600 ml (20 fl oz/2½ cups) club soda

1 Light the barbecue (grill). Halve the grapefruit. Pour a tablespoon of sugar onto each cut edge and press it in with your fingers. Wait a few minutes to allow the sugar to dissolve into the juice. Place the grapefruit halves onto the barbecue, cut-side down, directly above the charcoal. Ideally, there should be flames so that the sugar and pulp char slightly.

2 Using a citrus reamer, press the juice out of the charred grapefruit into a mixing bowl. Add the beetroot juice and mezcal, and mix.

3 Prepare drinking glasses. Add ice and pour around 170 ml (6 fl oz/¾ cup) from the mixing bowl into each glass. Top with 100 ml (3½ fl oz/scant ½ cup) club soda, mix gently and serve.

GARNISH LIKE A PRO **Why not garnish with a piece of the grilled grapefruit? All you have to do is cut a small slice off the grilled part before squeezing out the juice.**

BLACK BEAN AND KING OYSTER MUSHROOM BURGER

Serves 6

rapeseed (canola) oil or peanut oil, for frying

60 g (2 oz) finely chopped yellow onion

1 teaspoon Tabasco, or Midsummer's Louisiana Hot
    Sauce, p. 171

3 tablespoons HP sauce or other brown sauce
    (steak sauce)

2 large king oyster mushrooms

50 g (2 oz) walnuts, peeled
    and chopped

mild chilli powder, e.g. piment d'Espelette

150 g (5 oz/2½ cups) cooked black beans

2 tablespoons finely chopped parsley leaves

40 g (1½ oz/scant ½ cup) cooked beluga lentils

300 g (10½ oz/3⅓ cups) cooked porridge (oatmeal)

sea salt flakes

To serve

2–3 red (bell) peppers

1 tablespoon olive oil

6 burger buns, halved

1 tablespoon unsalted butter

6 eggs

6 tablespoons mayonnaise

parsley leaves

1. Heat some rapeseed or peanut oil in a frying pan (skillet) and fry the onions on a fairly high heat until they have browned thoroughly and are almost on the verge of being burnt. Lower the heat, mix in the Tabasco and HP sauce and take the frying pan off the heat.

2. Cut the mushrooms into ½ cm (¼ in) cubes. Warm plenty of oil in a frying pan on medium heat. Add the mushrooms and fry until soft, for around 20 minutes. Drain the oil.

3. Toast the walnuts in a dry cast-iron pan on a medium heat until they begin to colour, for around 2 minutes. Shake the pan occasionally to make sure the nuts don't burn too much. However, it doesn't matter if they take on a lot of colour. Remove the pan from the heat and season with chilli and salt.

4. Place the walnuts in a bowl together with the beans, parsley, lentils, porridge, mushrooms and a pinch of salt. Mix together using a potato masher (the beans should only be slightly mashed). Add the onion mixture and stir to ensure that everything is mixed.

5. Shape the batter into six round patties – either by hand or by using a shaper. Place them on a plate and cover with cling film (plastic wrap). Leave them to stand in the refrigerator for at least 1 hour – preferably longer – so that they hold together better when being grilled.

6. Light the barbecue (grill) and grill the peppers hard so that they turn black on the outside. I usually place the peppers onto the barbecue while the fire is still burning – preferably on top of a wood-burning fire. Put the peppers in a plastic bag and leave to cool for around 10 minutes. Rub the skin off by massaging the peppers while they are still in the bag. Cut into even strips.

7. Heat a few tablespoons of olive oil in a cast-iron pan, either on the hob or on the barbecue. Fry the patties on a medium heat for a few minutes on each side. Then place them on the barbecue in indirect heat, close the lid and roast for 10–15 minutes.

8. Brush the cut surface of the buns with olive oil and grill them quickly on the barbecue.

9. Dry out the cast-iron pan, then add in a tablespoon of butter. Return it to the grill and fry the eggs.

10. Add a generous tablespoon of mayonnaise to each bun and place the burger on top. Top with the grilled pepper, parsley and the fried egg.

COURGETTE AND MUNG BEAN BURGER
with sriracha mayonnaise and furikake

Serves 6

200 g (7 oz) yellow onions, finely chopped

2 tablespoons rapeseed (canola) oil

150 g (5 oz/⅔ cup) cooked rice

200 g (7 oz) courgette (zucchini)

300 g (10½ oz) mung beans, cooked

50 g (2 oz/scant ½ cup) buckwheat flour

1 tablespoon Korean dried red pepper

1 tablespoon sesame seeds

1 teaspoon virgin coconut oil

1 teaspoon toasted sesame oil

1 pinch of Chinese five spice

To serve

6 burger buns, halved

unsalted butter

salad leaves

spring onions (scallions), finely chopped

bean sprouts

6 tablespoons Sriracha Mayonnaise, see recipe
    on p. 166

6 teaspoons Furikake, see recipe on p. 170

1 Place the onions in a cold saucepan together with a tablespoon of the rapeseed oil. Put the saucepan on a medium heat and cover with the lid. The onions will quickly start to release moisture and by letting them cook in their liquid, the flavour will be concentrated. Stir using a wooden spoon around every 5 minutes for a total of 30 minutes.

2 Add the onions and rice to a food processor and pulse until smooth.

3 Cut the courgette into thin batons. Place them in a bowl together with the onion and rice mix and the rest of the ingredients. Mix together using a wooden spoon or your hands (the beans should only be slightly mashed).

4 Heat a frying pan (skillet) and add the remaining tablespoon of rapeseed oil. Lift a little batter at a time into the frying pan using a large spoon and shape into small patties. Fry for around 1 minute on each side so that they take on a little colour. If you like, you can use a shaper at the very beginning to make sure the patties retain their shape better. Place the shaper into the frying pan and fill with the batter. When cooked, place the patties on a baking sheet and leave to cool. Cover with cling film (plastic wrap) and leave in the refrigerator for at least 1 hour so that they set.

5 Light the barbecue (grill) and let the charcoal take on a strong, even glow. Butter the buns on the cut surface and grill them quickly on the barbecue. Then quickly grill the patties on either side so that they warm up and get an even crispier surface.

6 Add a few salad leaves to each bun and place a patty on top. Add the spring onions, bean sprouts, a tablespoon of Sriracha Mayonnaise and top with the Furikake.

HARISSA-MARINATED AUBERGINE BURGER
with baba ghanoush and dukkah

Serves 6

2 medium aubergines (eggplants), about 600 g
(1 lb 5 oz)

Harissa marinade

4 tablespoons rapeseed (canola) oil

2 tablespoons Harissa, see recipe on p.171

1 pinch of ground cumin

juice of 1 lime

1 tablespoon cane sugar

1 garlic clove

Baba ghanoush

2 medium aubergines (eggplants), about 600 g
(1 lb 5 oz)

2 garlic cloves, with the skin on

juice of ½ lemon

1 teaspoon mild chilli powder, e.g. piment d'Espelette

100 ml (3½ fl oz/scant ½ cup) olive oil + a little
extra for serving

sea salt flakes

To serve

6 burger buns, halved

1 tablespoon olive oil

1 unwaxed lime, finely zested

Dukkah, see recipe on p.168

1 Mix all the marinade ingredients together using a hand-held blender or food processor.

2 Cut the aubergines into slices 1 cm (½ in) thick (try to make the slices as even as possible). Pour the Harissa marinade into a plastic bag and add the aubergine slices. Rub the aubergine through the bag so the marinade is evenly distributed. Leave to rest in the refrigerator for 7–8 hours. Take it out a few times and rub the aubergine or shake the bag to ensure it is evenly coated.

3 Light the charcoal in the barbecue (grill). Continue making the baba ghanoush. Pierce the aubergines in a few places using a cocktail stick (toothpick) and then place them straight onto the glowing charcoal in the barbecue, even if the charcoal is still burning. Grill the aubergines until the skin has charred completely and the aubergine is soft inside, around 15 minutes. Add the garlic when there is 5–10 minutes left and grill them until they are also soft inside. Set the garlic and aubergine aside until they are cool enough to handle.

4 Cut the aubergines lengthways and remove the flesh with a spoon (try to remove as much flesh as possible). Halve the garlic and scoop out the flesh. Place the garlic and aubergine flesh into a large mixing bowl. Add the lemon juice, chilli powder and a little olive oil, and mix using a whisk. Add the rest of the oil, a little at a time, while mixing vigorously. If you prefer a firmer consistency, reduce the amount of oil used. Season with salt.

5 Remove the aubergine slices from the marinade, place them on paper towels and dry the cut edges. Add the aubergine slices to wooden skewers and grill on the barbecue. Turn them occasionally and brush with a little more marinade. Once the aubergines start to take on a nice, caramelised golden-brown colour, they are done. Set aside and brush again with the marinade.

6 Brush the buns with olive oil on the cut surface and grill them quickly on the barbecue.

7 Add 2–3 slices of aubergine to each bun, dollop 2 generous tablespoons of baba ghanoush on top, grate some lime zest over and top with Dukkah.

31

Table barbecues are common in both Japan and Korea. They are designed to provide a good, even heat. They usually get very hot, so keep an eye on what you are grilling. Put ingredients on a skewer or use tongs to ensure you can quickly turn things when necessary. An investment in a table barbecue is an investment in social grilling! They are great for gathering around and are also easy to handle and use.

HARISSA-MARINATED SWEET POTATO
with grilled cabbage leaves and black dukkah

Serves 6

2 medium sweet potatoes
120 g (4 oz) cabbage leaves
1 tablespoon rapeseed (canola) oil
1 pinch of salt

Harissa marinade

4 tablespoons rapeseed (canola) oil
2 tablespoons Harissa, see recipe on p.171
1 pinch of ground cumin
juice of 1 lime
1 tablespoon cane sugar
1 garlic clove

To serve

Black Dukkah, see recipe on p.168
oregano leaves
sea salt flakes

1 Mix all the marinade ingredients together using a hand-held blender or food processor.

2 Scrub the sweet potatoes under running water and dry thoroughly. Cut the sweet potatoes into slices around 1 cm (½ in) thick and place them on baking parchment. Brush them with the marinade, turn the slices over and brush the other side.

3 Light the charcoal in the table barbecue (grill) and let it take on a fine, soft glow. Grill the sweet potato slices on the barbecue, occasionally turning them over and brushing them with a little more marinade. Once the sweet potatoes start to take on a nice, caramelised golden-brown colour, they are done. Set aside and brush them with more marinade.

4 Place the cabbage leaves in a mixing bowl and massage in the oil and salt. Place the cabbage leaves on the barbecue – they will cook quickly, so have tongs or tweezers close at hand. Turn them a few times so that you can see the leaves taking on colour on both sides.

5 Place a few cabbage leaves on a plate, add a few slices of sweet potato on top and finish off with Black Dukkah, oregano and sea salt flakes.

SRIRACHA-MARINATED BROCCOLI
with shiitake mushroom and shiso broth

Serves 6

2 large heads of broccoli, about 300–400 g
    (10½–14 oz)

Marinade

3 tablespoons rapeseed (canola) oil

2 tablespoons tamari

1 tablespoon sriracha

1 teaspoon vinegar, 12 per cent

1 teaspoon light miso

1 teaspoon cane sugar

1 garlic clove

1 teaspoon toasted sesame oil

Shiitake mushroom and shiso broth

500 ml (17 fl oz/2 cups) water

20 g (¾ oz) dried shiitake mushrooms

6 cm (2½ in) leek, white part only

2 tablespoons cold-pressed rapeseed (canola) oil

4–5 fresh shiitake mushrooms, washed

2 garlic cloves, crushed with the skin on

2 tablespoons sake

1 tablespoon mirin

1 teaspoon freshly grated ginger root

4–5 Sichuan peppercorns

1 cm (½ in) strip unwaxed lime peel

500 ml (17 fl oz/2 cups) Vegetable Stock,
    see recipe on p. 162

2 large shiso leaves

To serve

broccoli florets

2 tablespoons oregano leaves

2 tablespoons small shiso leaves

1 tablespoon finely chopped green chilli

6 teaspoons sesame oil

1 Mix all the marinade ingredients together using a hand-held blender or food processor.

2 Start by cutting the small florets of broccoli off the stalk using a knife. Set aside. Now cut the stalk into four pieces lengthways then cut these batons in four in the opposite direction.

3 Put the pieces of broccoli stalk on a skewer, brush with marinade and put on a plate.

4 Boil the water for the broth. Put the dried mushrooms in a mixing bowl. Pour over the boiling water, cover with a lid and leave for 20 minutes. Drain the mushrooms (reserving the liquid), dry them on paper towels and set aside. Cut the leeks into thin strips. Pour the rapeseed oil into a stainless steel saucepan on a medium heat. Add the leeks and fry until they are soft, around 10 minutes. Add the fresh mushrooms and garlic and fry while stirring for around 5 minutes. Add the rest of the ingredients except for the shiso leaves. Mix well. Raise the heat, add the mushroom broth and bring to the boil so that it reduces slightly, around 10 minutes. Remove the pan from the heat and add the shiso leaves. Leave to stand, covered with a lid, for a further 20 minutes. Strain the broth into a second saucepan and keep warm.

5 Light the charcoal in the table barbecue (grill) and let it take on a soft glow. Barbecue the broccoli skewers directly on the charcoal, without using a grill, turning them often. Brush occasionally with more marinade. Once the broccoli starts to become caramelised they are done. Set aside and brush again.

6 Pour around 100 ml (3½ fl oz/scant ½ cup) of broth onto each plate. Add a skewer, top with the reserved small broccoli florets, herbs and chilli. Drizzle toasted sesame oil on top.

APPLE AND BRUSSELS SPROUTS SKEWERS
with whisky-pickled mustard seeds

Serves 6

5 small apples, quartered

18 Brussels sprouts

4 unwaxed lemons

6 tablespoons melted unsalted butter

3 teaspoons cane sugar

To serve

Whisky-pickled Mustard Seeds, see recipe on p. 174

1 Put 3 pieces of apple and 3 Brussels sprouts onto each wooden skewer. Squeeze some juice from one of the lemons onto the apple pieces to stop them turning brown. Place the skewers on a baking sheet and brush them with butter.

2 Light the charcoal in the table barbecue (grill) and let it take on a fine, soft glow. Barbecue the apple and Brussels sprout skewers directly on the charcoal, without using a grill, initially turning them often since it is so hot. Brush them occasionally with more butter. Once the apples begin to take on a nice, caramelised golden-brown colour and the Brussels sprouts are somewhat burnt, they are ready. Set aside and brush again with butter.

3 Place on the grill. Halve the remaining 3 lemons and sprinkle sugar on the cut edges. Use your fingers to press the sugar into the flesh of the fruit. Grill the lemons with the cut edge facing down so that they turn golden brown and the sugar caramelises.

4 Place the skewer on a chopping board and sprinkle the Whisky-pickled Mustard Seeds on top. Serve alongside a half lemon.

HASSELBACK KING OYSTER MUSHROOMS

Serves 6

6 large king oyster mushrooms

6 Smoked Onions, see recipe on p. 172

Marinade

4 tablespoons rapeseed (canola) oil

1 tablespoon light miso

1 tablespoon tamari

juice of ½ lime

1 teaspoon honey

1 garlic clove

1 teaspoon sesame oil

Soup base

3 tablespoons smoked rapeseed (canola) oil from
    the onion halves above

70 g (2½ oz) finely chopped shallots

100 ml (3½ fl oz/scant ½ cup) sherry

200 ml (7 fl oz/scant 1 cup) Vegetable Stock,
    see recipe on p. 162

1 tablespoon light miso

600 ml (20 fl oz/2½ cups) almond milk

To serve

sea salt flakes

1 Mix all the marinade ingredients using a hand-held blender or food processor.

2 Put the mushrooms on a wooden skewer and make diagonal cuts into them at intervals of 4–5 mm (¼ in). Turn the mushrooms over and do the same on the other side. Brush with the marinade and place on a baking sheet.

3 Pour the smoked rapeseed oil into a cold saucepan, add the shallots and put on a medium heat. Stir constantly using a wooden spoon and cook until the shallots soften but without taking on any colour, around 10 minutes. Pour over the sherry, raise the heat and leave to cook for 5 minutes. Add the Vegetable Stock, miso and almond milk, reduce the heat and whisk thoroughly to ensure everything is mixed. Leave to simmer for a further 10 minutes. Remove from the heat and use a hand-held blender to blend the soup until smooth. Cover with a lid and set aside.

4 Light the charcoal in the table barbecue (grill) and let it take on a fine, soft glow. Barbecue the mushrooms directly on the charcoal, without using a grill, initially turning them often since it is so hot. Brush them occasionally with more marinade. Once the mushrooms take on a nice, caramelised golden-brown colour, they are done. Set aside and brush again. Add the grill to the table barbecue and grill the Smoked Onions so that they warm up and their skins are slightly burnt. Brush them with their own smoked oil and set aside.

5 Divide the soup between 6 bowls. Break apart the onions and add the pieces to the soup. Add a mushroom to each bowl and top with a little sea salt flakes.

TURNIP SKEWERS with grilled collard greens and sour tomato sauce

Serves 6

12 small turnips, halved

3 tablespoons rapeseed (canola) oil

300 g (10½ oz) collard greens or any type of leafy
    green, e.g. black or green kale

1 teaspoon salt

To serve

dill fronds

fennel flowers or fennel dill

mild chilli powder, e.g. piment d'Espelette

sea salt flakes

600 ml (20 fl oz/2½ cups) Fermented Yellow Tomato
    Sauce, see recipe on p. 164

1 Light the table barbecue (grill) and let the charcoal take on a strong, even glow.

2 Put 4 turnip halves onto each wooden skewer and brush them with rapeseed oil. Put them on the grill with the cut edge facing down and grill for 3–4 minutes, or until they begin to take on some colour. Turn them over and grill the other side for about the same amount of time – take care to ensure they don't burn. Wrap the skewer in foil and set aside.

3 Place the cabbage leaves in a small bowl and drizzle 2 tablespoons of oil over them. Sprinkle with the salt and massage the oil and salt into the leaves. Barbecue them on the grill or in a flour sifter (see tip on p. 94) until they turn crisp and take on some colour. Set aside.

4 Set out 6 bowls and place a fistful of leaves in the bottom of each one. Place a skewer on each bowl and top with dill, fennel flowers or fennel dill, the chilli powder and salt. Serve with the Fermented Yellow Tomato Sauce alongside.

SANGRITAS made with grilled chillies and sour beer

Makes 6 drinks

12 red chillies (strength according to preference)

1 teaspoon sea salt flakes

½ teaspoon coriander seeds

½ teaspoon black peppercorns

240 ml (8½ fl oz/1 cup) tomato juice

To serve

6 teaspoons mild chilli powder, e.g. piment
    d'Espelette

3 teaspoons salt

1 wedge of lime

ice

1.2 litres (40 fl oz/4¾ cups) sour beer, preferably
    a fruity variety based on citrus fruits or berries

6 shots of mezcal, 60 ml (2 fl oz/¼ cup) each

1 Light the table barbecue (grill) and grill the chillies while the fire is still burning so that their skins blacken. Place the chillies in a plastic bag with the salt and let them steam in their own heat. Once they have cooled down, after 10–15 minutes, rub the skin off by massaging the chillies while they are still in the bag. Remove the chillies from the bag and split them lengthways. Remove the seeds and set aside.

2 Heat a cast-iron pan on a medium heat. Toast the reserved chilli seeds, coriander seeds and black peppercorns until the seeds turn golden brown and release their aroma. Crush them coarsely using a pestle and mortar.

3 Place the chillies and spices together with the tomato juice and blend until smooth, using a hand-held blender or food processor. Strain into a mixing bowl.

4 Mix the chilli powder with the salt and put on a plate. Prepare drinking glasses by running the wedge of lime along a quarter of the rim of the glass and then dipping that part into the chilli and salt mix. Add ice to each glass and pour around 50 ml (1¾ fl oz/3 tablespoons) from the bowl into each one. Add 200 ml (7 fl oz/scant 1 cup) of sour beer and stir gently. Serve alongside a shot of mezcal.

ALEX'S FERMENTED POTATO TORTILLAS

Serves 6

Fermented potatoes

600 g (1 lb 5 oz) large potatoes

9 g (2 teaspoons) salt, without iodine

Potato tortillas

500 g (1 lb 2 oz) fermented potatoes (including
the liquid that is formed)

25 g (1 oz/¼ cup) organic rye flour

175 g (6 oz/1½ cups) organic plain (all-purpose)
flour

rapeseed (canola) oil

1 Start with the fermented potatoes. Set the oven to 180°C (350°F/gas 6). Bake the potatoes for around 1 hour. Remove the potatoes from the oven and set aside until they are cool enough to handle. Hollow out the potatoes and place the flesh in a mixing bowl, you should get around 500 g (1 lb 2 oz).

2 Add the salt – it should be 1.8 per cent of the weight of the potatoes in the bowl. Mix without mashing the potatoes too much – there should be some big bits left. Place the mixture into ziplock bags and remove as much air as possible. Leave the bags at room temperature for 3–4 days. They will expand slightly, and liquid will be released. Turn them over occasionally during the process.

3 After 3–4 days at room temperature, the lactic acid bacteria will have eaten up all the available sugar and the potatoes will be fermented. You can either make the dough straight away, or store the potatoes in the refrigerator until you need them. You can also freeze the fermented potatoes to use much later on.

4 Pour the fermented potatoes, including all the liquid, into a mixing bowl and add the flour a little at a time. Some types of flour bind with liquid more than others, so use trial and error to find the right amount. Mix the dough with your hands or use a potato masher to begin with to mash the bigger bits of potato then shape the dough into a ball. It will be fairly sticky, but should still hold together well. If it seems dry, add a little water at intervals until it is nice and soft.

5 Split the dough into smaller pieces and roll these into small balls, about 2 cm (¾ in) in diameter. Place them on a plate with plenty of rye flour to stop them from sticking together. Leave to rest for around 10 minutes.

6. Cut out a sheet of baking parchment that is slightly larger than your tortilla press. Take a sheet of baking parchment and position it in the press, drip a little oil in the middle of the parchment and place the ball on top. Take another sheet of parchment, drip a little oil on it and then position it on top of the ball. Press it gently to ensure it stays in place when you close the press. Press the ball into a tortilla about 2 mm (⅛ in) thick.

7. While still between the sheets of paper, place the tortilla in a dry, warm – verging on hot – frying pan (skillet). Fry for 30 seconds, turn over and remove the paper from the fried side. Fry the other side for 30 seconds, turn it over again and remove the second sheet of paper.

8. Remove the tortilla and place it between two dish towels while you make the rest. I usually run a couple of frying pans at once. You have to experiment a little on the frying pan temperature until you find a level where the tortillas speckle and puff up a bit without getting burnt.

TACOS with black mole, smoked tomatoes, coriander root and cotija cheese

Serves 6

Black mole

1 tomato, halved

100 g (3½ oz) sourdough bread

30 g (1 oz) crushed pecans

2 tablespoons almonds, crushed

1 tablespoon rapeseed (canola) oil

50 g (2 oz) dried ancho chillies

50 g (2 oz) dried chipotle chillies

2 small yellow onions, quartered

2 garlic cloves, finely chopped

1 teaspoon dried thyme

1 teaspoon dried oregano

2 tablespoons black sesame seeds

1 pinch of cinnamon

5 black peppercorns

1 pinch of freshly grated nutmeg

4 cloves

1 teaspoon freshly grated ginger root

130 g (4 oz) dark raisins

400 ml (13 fl oz/generous 1½ cups) Vegetable Stock, see recipe on p. 162

To serve

6 Fermented Potato Tortillas, see recipe on p. 46

18 small smoked tomatoes

coriander (cilantro), picked leaves and finely chopped roots (I usually buy whole coriander with roots in Asian grocery stores – the roots of those grown in pots are too slender)

60 g (2 oz) Cotija, or another hard cheese such as pecorino or Parmesan

1. Start with the mole. Light the table barbecue (grill) and let the charcoal take on a fine, soft glow. Grill the tomato halves with the cut edge facing down until the outside has blackened somewhat.

2. Tear the bread into small pieces and place together with the pecans and almonds in a dry cast-iron pan and put on the barbecue. Drip a little oil on top and shake the pan occasionally to ensure everything toasts evenly, around 5–10 minutes. Place the mixture in a mixing bowl and set aside.

3. Slice open the chillies and remove the seeds – set these aside. Place the chillies in a food processor and blend until a powder. Set aside. Put the reserved chilli seeds in the cast-iron pan and toast them until they are burnt and completely black, around 5 minutes. Put the burnt seeds in a bowl and pour 200 ml (7 fl oz/scant 1 cup) of cold water over them. Leave to stand for 1½ hours. Strain and set aside.

4. Return the cast-iron pan to the barbecue to a spot where the temperature is lower. Pour in the oil, add the onions and tomato and leave to simmer for 15 minutes. Stir occasionally. Add the garlic and simmer for a further 10 minutes.

5. Then add the thyme, oregano, sesame seeds, cinnamon, peppercorns, nutmeg, cloves, ginger and raisins. Stir for 2–3 minutes to ensure that everything is well mixed. Add the bread and nut mix, chilli powder, chilli seeds and Vegetable Stock and cook for around 10 minutes.

6. Pour the mole into a food processor and blend until smooth. Pour everything back into the cast-iron pan and leave to cook for a further 30 minutes. Stir occasionally to ensure it does not burn. Add a little water if it gets too dry.

7. Place a Tortilla on each plate and dollop 2 tablespoons of mole onto each one. Top with three smoked tomatoes, coriander and finish by grating the cheese over it.

TACOS WITH GRILLED AVOCADO, PICKLED RED ONIONS AND CHILLI SAUCE

Serves 6

3–4 medium avocados
juice of 1 lime
rapeseed (canola) oil

To serve
6 Fermented Potato Tortillas, see recipe on p. 46
Pickled Red Onions, see recipe on p. 162
hot chilli sauce, e.g. Midsummer's Louisiana Hot
    Sauce, see recipe on p. 171

1 Light the table barbecue (grill) and let the charcoal take on a strong, even glow. Halve the avocados and remove the stones. Carefully hollow them out using a spoon and then cut the biggest possible slices lengthways, around 1 cm (⅓ in) thick. Place the slices on a plate and brush them with lime juice and then oil.

2 Grill the avocado slices quickly on a really high heat. The outsides should be caramelised and almost burnt, while inside the avocados should be cold and retain their consistency.

3 Place a Tortilla on each plate and top with a few slices of avocado. Finish with Pickled Red Onions and drizzle a little chilli sauce on top according to your preference.

TACOS WITH KING OYSTER MUSHROOMS AND PINEAPPLE

Serves 6

3 large king oyster mushrooms, torn into long
    pieces
1 tablespoon rapeseed (canola) oil
6 pieces of Roasted Pineapple, see recipe
    on p. 74, steps 1 and 3

Mushroom spice
1½ teaspoons salt
2 teaspoons mild chilli powder, e.g. piment
    d'Espelette
1 teaspoon onion powder
1 teaspoon garlic powder
1 teaspoon smoked paprika
1 pinch of cumin
1 pinch of cayenne pepper

To serve
6 Fermented Potato Tortillas, see recipe on p. 46
6 lime wedges

1. Light the table barbecue (grill) and let the charcoal take on a strong, even glow. Mix all the mushroom spice ingredients in a bowl.

2. Place the mushrooms in a bowl with the oil and mix until all the pieces are covered. Sprinkle most of the spice over and fold into the mushrooms carefully. Place the mushrooms in a double strainer (see tip on p. 56) and put on the grill or hold it over the glow. Occasionally shake the strainer, and drip a little oil on at intervals. Open after a few minutes and check whether the mushrooms have taken on any colour, cooking until golden brown. Set aside.

3. Place a Tortilla on each plate, top with pineapple on one side and the mushrooms on the other, season with mushroom spice and serve with a lime wedge.

49

FENNEL ROOT with shiitake mushrooms, spring onions, buckwheat and herb oil

Serves 6

300 g (10½ oz) fennel roots

1 litre (34 fl oz/4 cups) water

1 teaspoon sea salt flakes

juice of ½ lemon

300 g (10½ oz) shiitake mushrooms

4 tablespoons rapeseed (canola) oil

Herb oil

4 tablespoons parsley leaves

4 tablespoons mint leaves + 2 tablespoons
   for serving

2–3 tarragon leaves

1 garlic clove

juice of ½ lemon

3 tablespoons olive oil

sea salt flakes and black pepper

Boiled buckwheat

700 ml (24 fl oz/scant 3 cups) water

150 g (5 oz/scant 1 cup) whole buckwheat

2 teaspoons herbal salt

1 sprig of parsley

Grilled and steamed spring onions

3 tablespoons olive oil

6 spring onions (scallions)

sea salt flakes and black pepper

1. Scrub and scrape the fennel roots clean. Place them in a bowl with the water, salt and lemon juice. Cover with cling film (plastic wrap) and leave in the refrigerator overnight.

2. Make the herb oil by mixing the herbs, garlic, lemon juice and olive oil using a hand-held blender or food processor. Season with salt and pepper to taste.

3. Boil the water for the buckwheat in a saucepan. Rinse the buckwheat in a sieve (fine-mesh strainer), first in hot water and then cold. Reduce to a low heat, then add the buckwheat, salt and parsley. Cook for 10 minutes, stirring occasionally. Remove from the heat and leave to stand and swell for 15 minutes.

4. Light the table barbecue (grill). Pour olive oil into a plastic bag big enough to accommodate the spring onions and keep near to the barbecue. Season the spring onions with salt and pepper and put them on the barbecue while the charcoal is still burning. Grill the spring onions so that the surface is slightly burnt. Remove the spring onions using tongs and place in the plastic bag. Knot the bag and shake it so that the oil covers all of the spring onions. Leave the spring onions in the bag for around 20 minutes so that they are steamed in their own heat.

5. Clean the shiitake mushrooms and cut up larger mushrooms so that all pieces are about the same size. Place them in a bowl with 1½ tablespoons of rapeseed oil and a little salt and pepper, and mix to ensure they are properly covered. Place the mushrooms in a double strainer (see tip on p. 56) and put this on the barbecue or hold it over the glow. Occasionally shake the strainer, and drip a little oil on at intervals. Open after a few minutes and check whether the mushrooms have taken on any colour. They will be done when they turn a lovely golden brown. Set aside.

6. Remove the fennel roots from the water and dry them. Repeat the same procedure as with the mushrooms in step 5.

7. Spoon some buckwheat onto each plate, followed by a few fennel roots, some shiitake mushrooms and a spring onion split lengthways. Top with herb oil and fresh mint.

GRILLED PIMIENTOS DE PADRÓN
with crème fraîche and grated kombu

Serves 6

300 g (10½ oz) pimientos de Padrón

2 tablespoons rapeseed (canola) oil

sea salt flakes

300 ml (10 fl oz/1¼ cups) crème fraîche

2 teaspoons mild chilli powder, e.g. piment
    d'Espelette

1 teaspoon sesame seeds (preferably a mixture
    of colours)

kombu leaves (available from Asian grocery stores)

1 Light the table barbecue (grill) and let the charcoal take on a fine, even glow.

2 Place the chillies in a bowl, cover with oil and massage until everything is covered. Place the chillies in a coarse mesh strainer and grill until they take on colour and their skin starts to bubble and crack. Remove from the grill and season with sea salt flakes to taste.

3 Dollop crème fraîche onto a plate, sprinkle chilli powder and sesame seeds on top and grate the kombu over it using a zester. Place the chillies on top and serve immediately.

USE A DOUBLE STRAINER FOR SMALL INGREDIENTS **To ensure that smaller ingredients such as Padrón chillies and mushrooms don't fall through the grill, use a double strainer. Take two equal sized, coarse mesh strainers, put what you want to grill inside and wrap the two handles together tightly using steel wire.**

FRENCH STRING BEANS with charcoal-roasted shallots and crème fraîche with garlic and herbs

Serves 6

18 shallots, with the skin on

600 g (1 lb 5 oz) French string beans

2 tablespoons rapeseed (canola) oil

Crème fraîche with herb oil

10 g (½ oz) fresh mixed chopped herbs,
    e.g. oregano, thyme and dill

2 garlic cloves

juice of ½ lemon

3 tablespoons olive oil

sea salt flakes and black pepper

200 ml (7 fl oz/scant 1 cup) crème fraîche

To serve

sea salt flakes

1 Start with the herb oil. Mix the herbs, garlic, lemon juice and olive oil using a hand-held blender or food processor. Season with salt and pepper to taste.

2 Add charcoal or firewood to half the barbecue (grill) so that you have space to roast the onions using indirect heat later. Light the barbecue and once it is burning strongly, place the shallots straight onto the charcoal so that the outer layer burns. Pick up the shallots, place on the grill and position them on the charcoal-free side. Close the lid and roast them using indirect heat for 20–30 minutes until the shallots are soft all the way through. You can measure the core temperature – it should preferably be above 60°C (140°F). Set aside and leave to cool.

3 Trim and wash the beans. Dry them and place in a bowl with the rapeseed oil. Mix well so that everything is covered in the oil. Place the beans on the barbecue straight over the glow and roll them back and forth constantly for around 5 minutes, taking care to ensure they don't burn too much. Remove them from the grill.

4 Pour crème fraîche into a bowl and drizzle two thirds of the herb oil over it at the same time as stirring it gently using a fork to ensure lovely marbling on the surface.

5 Press the shallots out of their burnt skins and cut them in half. Place them together with the beans on a plate. Drizzle the rest of the herb oil over and top with some sea salt flakes. Serve alongside the crème fraîche .

61

CHARCOAL-ROASTED POINTED CABBAGE
with browned butter and Béarnaise sauce

Serves 6

2 medium pointed cabbage heads (preferably red
    as they look best)

Béarnaise sauce

about 30 ml (1 fl oz/⅛ cup) water

2 tablespoons + 1 tablespoon white wine vinegar

1 small shallot, coarsely chopped with the skin on

1 sprig of tarragon

2 white peppercorns

2 Sichuan peppercorns

4 coriander seeds

300 g (10½ oz) unsalted butter

2 egg yolks, at room temperature

To serve

150 g (5 oz) unsalted butter

6 small sprigs of tarragon

1 Add charcoal or firewood to half the barbecue (grill) so that you have space to roast the cabbage using indirect heat later. Light the barbecue and once it is burning strongly, place the cabbage straight onto the charcoal so that the outer layer burns. Turn several times using tongs then remove from the charcoal. Place the grill on top and position the cabbage on its side away from the flames. Close the lid and roast using indirect heat for 1 hour until the cabbage feels soft when you gently press the skin. You can measure the core temperature – it should preferably be above 75°C (170°F).

2 Add the water, vinegar, shallots, tarragon and spices to a saucepan. Bring to the boil and reduce to half the volume. Drain the water and set aside for now. Prepare a water bath. Boil the water in a saucepan, then remove from the heat and cover with a stainless steel mixing bowl. Melt the butter in a saucepan so that it reaches a temperature of around 50°C (120°F). Pour the egg yolks into the mixing bowl, add the vinegar reduction and start to whisk. Add the butter in a thin and steady stream while whisking continuously. Once you obtain a good, thick consistency you can stir in a tablespoon of vinegar towards the end to add a little more acidity to the sauce.

3 Brown the butter for serving. Put a saucepan on a medium heat. Add the butter and start to whisk it just as it melts. Continue to whisk until the butter is lovely and golden brown in colour and smells nutty. Remove from the heat and continue to whisk for a little bit to avoid it burning on the bottom.

4 After the cabbage has cooled slightly, peel away the outermost burnt layers. Cut up the cabbage into portions and plate up. Spoon over the brown butter, dollop a little Béarnaise sauce over the top and garnish with sprigs of tarragon.

LEEK four ways

Serves 6

Pickled leek

100 ml (3½ fl oz/scant ½ cup) vinegar, 12 per cent
180 g (6 oz/scant 1 cup) caster (superfine) sugar
300 ml (10 fl oz/1¼ cups) water for the syrup +
    500 ml (17 fl oz/2 cups) for blanching
1 leek
100 g (3½ oz/⅓ cup) salt

Leek ash

leftover parts from the pickled leek

Grilled leek

2 large leeks

Leek and parsley mayonnaise

100 ml (3½ fl oz/scant ½ cup) olive oil
leftover parts of the leek from the grilled leek
10 g (½ oz) parsley leaves
400 ml (13 fl oz/generous 1½ cups) Mayonnaise
    with Eggs, see p. 166

To serve

6 teaspoons toasted sesame oil
6 tablespoons finely chopped cashews
sea salt flakes

1 Start with the pickled leek – it needs 24 hours in the refrigerator. Boil the vinegar, sugar and 300 ml (10 fl oz/1¼ cups) of water in a saucepan. Wash and remove the outer layer of the leek, save the green parts for making ash. Cut the leek into slices ½ cm (¼ in) thick and press out the leek rings as much as possible. Boil 500 ml (17 fl oz/2 cups) of water in a saucepan with the salt. Blanch the leek rings in the hot water for a few seconds then drain in a colander and rinse the leeks under cold running water. Place the leeks in a bowl and pour the syrup over, cover with a lid or cling film (plastic wrap) and put in the refrigerator.

2. Set the oven to the highest temperature. Take the leftover green parts from the leeks and cut them into long, thin, flat pieces. Place them on a baking sheet and put in the oven for a few minutes until the leeks are completely black. Remove the baking sheet and turn over the leaves. Return to the oven and let the other side turn black. Remove and leave to cool. Use a hand-held blender or food processor to blend the black leaves into a fine powder.

3. Add charcoal or firewood to half the barbecue (grill) so that you have space to roast the leeks using indirect heat later. Light the barbecue and once it is burning strongly, place the leeks on the grill or straight onto the charcoal so that the outer layer burns. Place the grill on top of the barbecue and position the leeks on the side away from the flames. Close the lid and roast using indirect heat for 20–30 minutes until the leeks are soft all the way through. You can measure the core temperature – it should preferably be above 85°C (185°F) in the middle.

4. Cut the leek into pieces as shown in the picture on the previous page, then set the diagonally cut pieces aside. Use the leftover pieces for the mayonnaise.

5. Warm up the olive oil on a medium heat in a saucepan, then add the leftover pieces of leek together with the parsley. Cook until soft, around 10 minutes. Pour everything into a food processor. Blend until smooth then pour the mixture into a mixing bowl and leave to cool. Add the mayonnaise and stir to ensure everything is well combined.

6. Place a piece of leek onto each plate. Drizzle a teaspoon of sesame oil, add some cashew crumbs along the sides and top with the pickled leeks. Sprinkle a few pinches of leek ash and dollop a generous spoonful of mayonnaise on top.

67

ROASTED CELERIAC with grilled chanterelles, chicory dukkah and herb cream

Serves 6

chicory (endive) leaves; alternatively dandelion,
    radicchio or other bitter leaves
sea salt flakes
2 tablespoons white wine vinegar
3 small celeriac (celery roots)

Herb cream
10 g (½ oz) fresh mixed herbs, e.g. thyme,
    rosemary and dill
juice of ½ lemon
3 tablespoons olive oil
salt and black pepper
100 ml (3½ fl oz/scant ½ cup) crème fraîche

Grilled chanterelles
150–200 g (5–7 oz) chanterelles
2–3 garlic cloves, lightly crushed
1 tablespoon rapeseed (canola) or peanut oil
salt and black pepper

To serve
Chicory Dukkah or ordinary Dukkah, see recipe on
    p.168
chicory (endive) flowers
sea salt flakes

1 Soak the chicory leaves in some salt and vinegar. Leave to stand until serving.

2 Add charcoal or firewood to half the barbecue (grill) so that you have space to roast the celeriac using indirect heat later. Light the barbecue and once it is burning strongly, place the celeriac onto the grill so that the outer layer burns. Then place the celeriac on the side away from the flames. Close the lid and roast using indirect heat for 1½ hours until the celeriac feels soft when you press the skin. You can measure the core temperature – it should preferably be above 60°C (140°F).

3 Make the herb cream. Using a hand-held blender or food processor, blend the herbs, lemon juice and olive oil. Season with salt and pepper to taste. Pour the herb mix into a mixing bowl, add the crème fraîche and mix thoroughly.

4 Trim and brush away any dirt from the chanterelles. Place them in a bowl together with the garlic. Add the rapeseed oil, season with salt and pepper and turn over. Then place the chanterelles in a double strainer (see tip on p. 56) and put this on the grill or hold it over the glow. Occasionally shake the strainer, and pour a little oil on at intervals. Open after a few minutes and check whether the mushrooms have taken on any colour. They will be done when they turn a lovely golden brown. Set aside for now.

5 Remove the chicory leaves from the water and dry them either using paper towels or with a salad spinner.

6 Peel the celeriac once they have cooled slightly. You can usually do this with your fingers, but you can otherwise cut the skin off using a knife. Try to keep as much as possible of the roasted vegetable just inside the skin intact. Cut each celeriac into four pieces.

7 Dollop a generous spoonful of herb cream onto each plate, sprinkle 2 tablespoons of Dukkah and add two pieces of celeriac to each. Top with chicory leaves and mushrooms. Garnish with the flowers or a suitable herb.

I often choose to roast larger, more compact vegetables or fruits until the skin is burnt and completely black, before cooking them using indirect heat for a little longer. This is an amazing way of producing the wonderful charred barbecue flavour while also cooking the insides without them drying out and getting boring, which can happen if you slice them and barbecue them.

ROASTED PINEAPPLE with rum coconut cream

Serves 6

2 medium pineapples

Rum coconut cream

1 vanilla pod (bean)

200 ml (7 fl oz/scant 1 cup) coconut cream

100 ml (3½ fl oz/scant ½ cup) crème fraîche

2 tablespoons dark rum

1 tablespoon cane sugar

To serve

1 unwaxed lime, finely zested

lemon verbena

1   Light the barbecue (grill). Pierce a few holes into each pineapple using a skewer and then place them straight onto the glowing charcoal – you can even do this while it is still burning. Roast the pineapple until the skin is completely charred and soft inside – this will take 1–2 hours or longer. The skin is very thick, so it can withstand being left for a while. You can tell it is almost done when the pineapple has shrunk slightly and the skin is slightly soft when you press it. You can measure the core temperature – it should preferably be above 80–90°C (175–195°F).

2   Make the cream while the pineapple is in the charcoal. Cut the vanilla pod lengthways and scrape the seeds into a bowl. Add the remaining ingredients and whip the cream as firmly as possible. I usually put it in the freezer for an hour before eating it so that it is extra firm when served.

3   First, cut the top off the pineapple and then set it upright. Cut off the outermost black skin, but try to keep as much of the brown flesh close to the skin as possible without too much of the charred layer remaining, then cut out quarters lengthways. I usually remove the core from the middle, which is often slightly too tough after being roasted for a long time.

4   Place two pieces of pineapple on each plate, dollop a generous tablespoon of coconut cream onto them and top with finely grated lime zest and lemon verbena.

SMOKY PINEAPPLE SOUR

Makes 6 drinks

300 g (10½ oz) Roasted Pineapple, see
    steps 1 and 3 in the recipe to the left
120 ml (4 fl oz/½ cup) agave syrup
1 teaspoon chopped green chilli
3 cm (1½ in) fresh ginger root, peeled
120 ml (4 fl oz/½ cup) freshly squeezed lime juice
600 ml (20 fl oz/2½ cups) pineapple juice
1 cinnamon stick, around 4 cm (1¾ in)
300 ml (10 fl oz/1¼ cups) gin
3 egg whites

To serve
smoke wood chips
ice
cinnamon stick
dried pineapple slices

1 Mix the charcoal-roasted pineapple, syrup, chilli, ginger, lime and pineapple juice in a food processor and pulse several times. Pour into a mixing bowl, add the cinnamon stick and leave in the refrigerator overnight.

2 Put the glasses in the refrigerator around an hour before serving the drinks. Strain the pineapple mix into a jug. Press hard to ensure you get a little of the pineapple flesh in the mixture.

3 Use a cocktail shaker big enough for two drinks. Add around 400 ml (13 fl oz/generous 1½ cups) of pineapple mixture, 100 ml (3½ fl oz/scant ½ cup) of gin and 1 egg white.

4 Shake once without ice to add air to the drink and let the egg white fluff up. Fill the shaker with ice and shake again until the shaker is cold.

5 Ignite some of the smoke wood chips and place on a baking sheet. Turn the glasses upside down and place over the chips so that smoke collects inside them. The cold glass will cool the smoke so that it stays in place when you turn them back over.

6 Turn the glasses over carefully so that you don't lose too much smoke. Add ice and slowly pour half of the liquid from the shaker, grate a little cinnamon and top with a slice of dried pineapple.

ROASTED AND SMOKED POTATOES with
beer-caramelised onions

Serves 6

6 medium potatoes (small baking potatoes)
100–200 g (3½–7 oz) applewood smoker chips

Caramelised onion mixture

6 medium yellow onions, chopped
3 tablespoons unsalted butter
200 ml (7 fl oz/scant 1 cup) beer, preferably lager

To serve

Pickled Wild Garlic Capers, see recipe on p. 175
oregano leaves
watercress
sea salt flakes

1 Add charcoal or firewood to half the barbecue (grill) so that you have space to roast the potatoes using indirect heat later. Light the barbecue and add a fistful of smoker chips to the glow once the flames have begun to die down. Place the potatoes on the grill on the side where there are no flames, cover with the lid and roast them using indirect heat for around 1 hour, turning them occasionally. The potatoes will be done when they feel soft when you gently touch the skin. You can measure the core temperature – it should preferably be above 90°C (195°F).

2 Place the onions and butter in a cold terrine dish or saucepan. Warm up on the grill on a medium heat and cover with a lid. The onions will soon start to release liquid and the flavours will be concentrated through the onions cooking in their own juices. Stir using a wooden spoon about every 5 minutes for 30–40 minutes. Take care to make sure it does not burn. (If you notice that it is getting too dry, you can add the beer earlier.) Add the beer, raise the heat and reduce the mixture substantially. Stir frequently, preferably towards the end when almost all the liquid has been reduced down – this should take around 20 minutes. Set the terrine to one side.

3 Cut an incision into each potato and squeeze the ends so that it opens up. Add a generous dollop of onions to each cut and top with Pickled Wild Garlic Capers, oregano, watercress and salt.

ROASTED SWEDE with grilled shiitake mushrooms and lovage broth

Serves 6

3 medium swedes
300 g (10½ oz) shiitake mushrooms

Lovage broth

1 litre (34 fl oz/4 cups) water
20 g (¾ oz) dried shiitake mushrooms
2 tablespoons cold-pressed rapeseed (canola) oil
300 g (10½ oz) peeled pearl onions
2 garlic cloves, crushed with the skin on
1 tablespoon white wine vinegar
2 bay leaves
1 white peppercorn
1 cm (½ in) strip of unwaxed lemon peel
2–3 sprigs of lovage

To serve

lovage leaves
1 tablespoon cold-pressed rapeseed (canola) oil
sea salt flakes and pepper

1 Add charcoal or firewood to half the barbecue (grill) so that you have space to roast the swede using indirect heat later. Light the barbecue and once it is burning strongly, place the swede straight onto the charcoal so that the outer layer burns. Turn several times using tongs. Place the grill on top and position the cabbage on its side away from the flames. Close the lid and roast using indirect heat for 1 hour until the swede feels soft when you gently press the skin. You can measure the core temperature – it should preferably be above 85°C (185°F) in the middle.

2 Boil the water for the broth. Put the dried mushrooms in a mixing bowl, cover in boiling water, then cover with a lid and leave to stand for 20 minutes. Strain the mushrooms and reserve the liquid. Dry the mushrooms using paper towels and set aside. Pour the oil into a stainless steel saucepan and put on a medium heat. Add the onions and fry until soft but without taking on any colour, around 10 minutes. Add the mushrooms and garlic and stir for around 5 minutes. Add the vinegar, bay leaves, peppercorn and lemon peel. Stir to ensure that everything is well combined. Raise the heat, add the reserved mushroom broth and bring to the boil so that it reduces slightly, around 10 minutes. Remove the pan from the heat, add the lovage and leave to stand covered with a lid for a further 20 minutes. Remove the pearl onions and set aside. Strain the rest of the broth into a second saucepan and keep it warm.

3 Trim and brush clean the fresh shiitake mushrooms. Grill them using a double strainer (see tip on p. 56) or fry them hard in a cast-iron pan with a little oil.

4 Peel the swede once it has cooled slightly. You can usually do this with your fingers, but you can otherwise cut the skin off using a knife. Try to keep as much as possible of the roasted vegetable just inside. Cut it into slices 3–4 mm (⅛ in) thick.

5 Place a few slices of swede in a soup bowl, cut the onions in four and place a few beside the swede. Pour over the broth, add a few shiitake mushrooms and lovage leaves. Drip a little cold-pressed rapeseed oil and season with salt and pepper.

79

ROASTED SWEDE ON A BED OF SHISO
with sour cream, horseradish and chervil

Serves 6

1 small swede
12 shiso or mint leaves
3 tablespoons sour cream
6 teaspoons freshly grated horseradish
6 chervil leaves
sea salt flakes

1 Add charcoal or firewood to half the barbecue (grill) so that you have space to roast the swede using indirect heat later. Light the barbecue and once it is burning strongly, place the swede straight onto the charcoal so that the outer layer burns. Turn several times using tongs. Place the grill on top and position the swede on its side away from the flames. Close the lid and roast using indirect heat for 1 hour until the swede feels soft when you gently press the skin. You can measure the core temperature – it should preferably be above 85°C (185°F).

2 Peel the swede once it has cooled slightly. You can usually do this with your fingers, but you can otherwise cut the skin off using a knife. Try to keep as much as possible of the roasted vegetable just inside.

3 Cut the swede into four and then cut into slices 3–4 mm (⅛ in) thick. Place the shiso leaves on plates and position a couple of slices of swede on top of each one. Dollop ½ tablespoon of sour cream onto each one, followed by 1 teaspoon of horseradish. Top with chervil leaves and a scattering of sea salt.

MAKE A DOUBLE BATCH **This is supposed to be a snack to go with your aperitif, but naturally you can double the recipe. They are usually popular, so don't be mean – make more!**

LOVE'S charcoal-roasted celeriac drink

Makes 6 drinks

2 medium celeriac (celery roots)

3 tablespoons unsalted butter

240 ml (8½ fl oz/1 cup) freshly squeezed lemon
    juice

100 ml (3½ fl oz/scant ½ cup) sugar syrup (1 part
    caster (superfine) sugar + 1 part water)

360 ml (12 fl oz/1½ cups) mezcal

ice

To serve

large ice cubes

1   Add charcoal or firewood to half the barbecue (grill) so that you have space to roast the celeriac using indirect heat later. Light the barbecue and once it is burning strongly, place the celeriac straight onto the charcoal so that the outer layer burns. Turn several times using tongs. Place the grill on top and position the celeriac on the grill on the charcoal-free side. Close the lid and roast using indirect heat for 1 hour until the celeriac feels soft when you gently press the skin. You can measure the core temperature – it should preferably be above 90°C (195°F).

2   Leave the celeriac to cool until you can handle them without burning yourself. Cut into four parts and then cut away the white flesh. If you can manage to get a little of the brown flesh just inside the black skin then that is great – there's lots of smoky flavour there.

3   Add the celeriac and butter to a food processor and blend until smooth.

4   Get out a cocktail shaker. For each drink, add 100 ml (3½ fl oz) of celeriac purée, 40 ml (3 tablespoons) of lemon juice, 15 ml (1 tablespoon) of sugar syrup and 60 ml (2 fl oz/¼ cup) of mezcal. Fill with ice cubes, attach the lid and shake away. Check whether it needs more acidity or sweetness, then adjust accordingly by either adding more lemon juice or sugar syrup.

5   Strain the drink into a glass filled with ice.

#3 CAST IRON AND CLAY POTS STRAIGHT IN THE FIRE

SALT-ROASTED RED BEETROOT
IN ONION SKINS

Serves 6

Grilled red onions

3 large red onions, halved with skin on

1 tablespoon rapeseed (canola) oil

1 tablespoon red wine vinegar, preferably
    merlot vinegar

1 pinch of dried oregano

1 teaspoon sea salt flakes

Salt-roasted beetroot

4 medium red beetroot

coarse sea salt

6–7 garlic cloves

thyme leaves

2 teaspoons olive oil

10 g (½ oz) finely chopped lemon balm

½ unwaxed lime, finely zested

Cep broth

1 litre (34 fl oz/4 cups) water

20 g (¾ oz) dried ceps

2 tablespoons cold-pressed rapeseed (canola) oil

2 yellow onions, peeled and quartered

2 garlic cloves, crushed with the skin on

1 tablespoon red wine vinegar, preferably
    merlot vinegar

2 bay leaves

1 black peppercorn

1 cm (½ in) strip unwaxed lime peel

2–3 sprigs of parsley

To serve

croutons

Whisky-pickled Mustard Seeds, see recipe on p. 174

lemon balm

1. Brush the onions with oil on the cut edge. Light the barbecue (grill) and place the onions, cut-side down, on the grill while there are still flames. Hold down using tongs until completely black. Place them in a plastic bag and add the vinegar, oregano and salt. Knot the bag tightly and leave the onions to steam.

2. Cover the bottom of a greased terrine or cast-iron pan with a layer of salt and position the beetroot with a little distance between them. Sprinkle with salt so they are almost covered. Insert the garlic and thyme between the beetroot. Position the terrine directly in the glowing charcoal and roast the beetroots until soft, around 40–50 minutes. When they look slightly shrunken and grey on the outside, they are usually perfectly cooked.

3. Boil the water for the broth. Put the mushrooms in a mixing bowl, cover in the boiling water, cover with a lid and leave to stand for 20 minutes. Strain the mushrooms and reserve the liquid. Dry the mushrooms using paper towels and set aside. Pour the rapeseed oil into a saucepan and put on a high heat. Add the onions and fry them hard for around 10 minutes until they take on colour. Add the mushrooms and garlic and fry while stirring for about 5 minutes. Mix in the vinegar, bay leaves, peppercorn and lime peel, and stir a few times to ensure everything is fully combined. Raise the heat, add the reserved mushroom broth and bring to the boil so that it reduces slightly, around 10 minutes. Remove the pan from the heat, add the parsley, and leave to stand covered with a lid for a further 20 minutes. Strain and set aside.

4. Peel the beetroot once they have cooled down slightly and cut them into cubes, around 5 x 5 mm (¼ x ¼ in). Place in a bowl with olive oil, lemon balm and finely grated lime zest and mix well.

5. Remove the onions from the bag and dry off the salt and oregano. Remove the larger outer layers of onion so that you have 'onion boats' to put the beetroot in – I usually get 3–4 from each onion half. Plate the 'onion boats', fill with the beetroot mixture and spoon a little broth over them so that the boats fill up. Top with croutons, the Whisky-pickled Mustard Seeds and a little lemon balm.

TARTE TATIN with sweet rye bread and walnuts

Serves 6

Pastry

220 g (8 oz/scant 2 cups) plain (all-purpose) flour

2 teaspoons baking powder

½ teaspoon salt

150 g (5 oz/¾ cup) cane sugar

200 g (7 oz/1 cup) unsalted butter, chilled

2 eggs

Topping

6 medium apples, peeled and cored

juice of ½ lemon

150 g (5 oz) sweetened rye bread

100 g (3½ oz) walnuts

150 g (5 oz/¾ cup) cane sugar

70 g (2½ oz/⅓ cup) unsalted butter

To serve

vanilla custard

1 Sift the flour and baking powder into a mixing bowl, then add the salt and sugar. Add the cold butter and rub it into the flour until it has a somewhat sandy consistency. Add the eggs and mix until the dough is lovely and soft. Cover in cling film (plastic wrap) and leave in the refrigerator for at least 30 minutes.

2 Cut the apples into thick wedges and place them in a mixing bowl with some lemon juice to stop them from going brown while you complete the other steps.

3 Put the bread and walnuts in a food processor and pulse so that they are well blended and finely chopped.

4 Light the barbecue (grill) and let the charcoal take on a strong, even glow. Put a cast iron saucepan on the grill, add the sugar and butter and melt together. Add the apple wedges and leave to simmer on a medium heat for around 15 minutes. Stir occasionally to ensure the apples do not stick.

5 Remove the pan from the heat and distribute the bread and walnut mixture over the apples.

6 Roll the dough out into a circle and place it on top of the apples as a loose lid. The edges should be a fair size and hang down the edge of the pan.

7 Place the pan back on the grill above indirect heat. Press the dough gently down onto the apples. Place the lid on the barbecue and bake for around 1 hour. Aim for a temperature of 150–170°C (300–340°F). Remove the pan and set aside.

8 Let the pie rest for a while until it has settled, then turn it out onto a serving plate. It's best when served with vanilla custard.

There are lots of types of charcoal with different characteristics, but generally the harder the charcoal the better the quality and the more evenly it burns. Japanese binchō-tan is the charcoal of choice of many barbecue geeks. It can maintain an excellent, even heat for many hours and is especially suitable for table barbecues (grills).

SALT-ROASTED PEARS with burrata and grilled black kale

Serves 6

6 medium pears

coarse sea salt

6–7 garlic cloves

thyme and oregano leaves

2–3 black kale

olive oil

3 burrata

sea salt flakes

To serve

olive oil

1–2 unwaxed lemons, finely zested

chive flowers or snipped chives

1 Light the barbecue (grill) and let the charcoal take on a strong, even glow.

2 Layer the bottom of a moist terrine dish or cast-iron pan with sea salt flakes and place the pears on the bed of salt at regular intervals from each other. Sprinkle with sea salt flakes so they are almost covered and insert the garlic and herbs between the pears.

3 Position the terrine directly on the glowing charcoal and roast the pears until soft, around 40–50 minutes. When the pears look slightly shrunken and golden brown on the outside, they are usually perfectly cooked on the inside.

4 Put the black kale leaves in a small bowl and drizzle with some oil. Sprinkle a little salt over them and massage into the leaves. Barbecue the leaves on the grill or in a flour sifter (as illustrated) until they turn crisp and take on some colour. Set aside.

5 Remove the pears from the salt bed and dry them off thoroughly. Halve them lengthways or quarter them, depending on size. Place a few pieces of pear on each plate and wrap in black kale. Halve the burrata and place a piece on top of each plate. Drizzle with a little olive oil, and top with finely zested lemon rind and a chive flower. If the flowers are out of season, snip some chives over the plate instead.

GRILLING DELICATE INGREDIENTS **When grilling vegetables or herbs and thin cabbage leaves that often fall between the grill or suffer too much in the heat, a flour sifter is a great option. Place it straight on the grill to add a little more distance between the ingredient and the heat, and use tongs or tweezers to turn delicate ingredients.**

#4 VEGETABLES ON CHARCOAL

CHARCOAL-ROASTED CARROTS with
lovage broth

Serves 6

6 medium carrots, preferably purple

Lovage broth

2 litres (70 fl oz/8 cups) Vegetable Stock, see
    recipe on p. 162

1 piece of fresh turmeric, about 3 cm (1¼ in), sliced
    with skin on

1 teaspoon black peppercorns

1 teaspoon coriander seeds

1 teaspoon Sichuan pepper

1 tablespoon white wine vinegar, preferably
    Champagne vinegar

1 sprig of lovage

sea salt flakes

To serve

lovage (not too much as it's a very strong, potent
    flavour)

parsley leaves

watercress

cold-pressed rapeseed (canola) oil

1   Start with the broth. Boil the Vegetable Stock together with the turmeric, peppercorns, coriander seeds and Sichuan pepper. Leave to cook for a few minutes then take off the heat. Add the vinegar and lovage. Stir a few times, cover with the lid and leave to stand for around 20 minutes. Strain and season with a little salt.

2   Add charcoal or firewood to half the barbecue (grill) so that you have space to roast the carrots using indirect heat later. Light the barbecue and once it is burning strongly, place the carrots straight onto the charcoal so that the outer layer burns. Turn several times using tongs. Pick up the carrots, place on the grill and position them on the charcoal-free side. Close the lid and roast using indirect heat for around 30 minutes. Remove using tongs and leave to cool.

3   Rub the skin off the carrots, either by using rubber gloves or with a plastic bag. Cut the carrots into slices around 1 cm (½ in) thick.

4   Plate the carrot slices, top with some herbs and finish with the broth and a few drops of a flowery, cold-pressed rapeseed oil.

CHARCOAL-ROASTED AUBERGINE with smoked tomatoes, grilled lemon and toasted pine nuts

Serves 6

6 medium aubergines (eggplants)

3 unwaxed lemons

400 ml (13 fl oz/generous 1½ cups) water

1 teaspoon salt

2–3 garlic cloves, crushed

1 sprig of parsley

1 sprig of lovage

1 teaspoon black peppercorns

1 teaspoon coriander seeds

12 Smoked Tomatoes + 2 tablespoons oil from the
 tomato smoking process, see recipe on p. 172

60 g (2 oz) pine nuts

To serve

1 sprig of parsley

1 Light the barbecue (grill). Pierce the aubergines in a few places using a cocktail stick (toothpick) then place them straight onto the glowing charcoal. This can even be done while the charcoal is still burning. Roast the aubergines until the skin has charred completely and the aubergine is soft inside, around 15 minutes. Place in a mixing bowl and cover with a lid or cling film (plastic wrap) so that they continue to steam and release some liquid.

2 Halve the lemons and grill them on the cut-side down until they have taken on some colour.

3 Peel the aubergines once they have cooled down enough to be handled without burning yourself. Try to retain as much of the brown flesh just beneath the skin as possible – this is where most of the flavour is – but ensure that all the charred skin is removed. Save the juice remaining in the mixing bowl for the broth in the next step.

4 Boil the water and salt in a saucepan, ensure that the salt dissolves into the water. Remove the pan from the heat. Add the garlic, parsley, lovage, peppercorns and coriander seeds. Add the leftover liquid from the aubergines and the smoked oil from the tomatoes. Cover with a lid and leave to stand for around 20 minutes. Strain the liquid.

5 Toast the pine nuts, either using a cast-iron pan or a sieve (fine-mesh strainer) above the fire (see tip on p. 56).

6 Place a piece of aubergine and 2 Smoked Tomatoes on each plate. Sprinkle a tablespoon of pine nuts on top. Pour over some broth, add a lemon half and top with parsley leaves.

CHARCOAL-ROASTED SAVOY CABBAGE
with lemon sauce and quail's egg

Serves 6

2 medium heads of savoy cabbage

6 quail's eggs

Lemon sauce

1 tablespoon rapeseed (canola) oil

1 tablespoon finely chopped garlic

1 tablespoon finely chopped shallot

2 tablespoons white wine

3 tablespoons freshly squeezed lemon juice

200 g (7 oz/1 cup) unsalted butter, cut into
    small cubes

To serve

3 small green chillies, finely sliced

oregano leaves

oxalis (wood sorrel)

1   Add charcoal or firewood to half the barbecue (grill) so that you have space to roast the cabbage using indirect heat later. Light the barbecue and, once it is burning strongly, place the savoy cabbages straight onto the charcoal so that the outer layer burns. Turn several times using tongs. Pick up the savoy cabbages, place on the grill and position them on the charcoal-free side. Close the lid and roast using indirect heat for around 1 hour until the cabbage feels soft when you gently press the skin. You can also measure the core temperature – it should be above 80°C (175°F) in the middle.

2   Pour the oil for the lemon sauce into a stainless steel saucepan and put on a medium heat. Add the garlic and shallots and fry until soft, but without taking on any colour. Add the white wine and lemon juice and leave to simmer for around 10 minutes. Strain to remove the shallots, then return the saucepan containing the liquid to the heat and lower the temperature slightly. Add half the butter and whisk thoroughly until the sauce begins to thicken. Add the rest of the butter and continue whisking until you have a lovely, creamy sauce.

3   Cut the tops off the quail's eggs and carefully pour the contents into the palm of your hand. Allow the egg white to run off and transfer the yolk to your dry hand before passing it back into the eggshell.

4   Remove the outermost burnt cabbage leaves once the cabbages are cool enough to handle. Then cut them into portion-sized pieces. Plate up the cabbage pieces and place the egg shell containing the yolk on top. Garnish with the chilli, oregano and oxalis. Serve the sauce alongside or drizzle it over the cabbage.

CHARCOAL-ROASTED LEEK with calypso beans, smoked onions and fennel broth

Serves 6

3 large leeks
150 g (5 oz/2½ cups) cooked kidney beans
4 Smoked Onions, see recipe on p. 172

Fennel broth

2 tablespoons rapeseed (canola) oil
1 yellow onion, coarsely chopped with the skin on
1 fennel bulb, coarsely chopped
2 garlic cloves, crushed with the skin on
the green parts of the leeks from above
    (around 200 g/7 oz)
2–3 sprigs of parsley
3 star anise
1 teaspoon white peppercorns
1 teaspoon salt
300 ml (10 fl oz/1¼ cups) water

To serve

fennel flowers or fennel dill

1 Start with the broth. Heat up the oil in a saucepan on a medium heat, add the onion and leave to simmer until it begins to soften. Add the rest of the ingredients except the water and fry while stirring – they should not take on any colour. Pour the water in after around 15 minutes and bring to the boil. Let the broth simmer for around 30 minutes so that it reduces down slightly. Strain and set aside.

2 Add charcoal or firewood to half the barbecue (grill) so that you have space to roast the leeks using indirect heat later. Light the barbecue and once it is burning strongly, place the leeks straight onto the charcoal so that the outer layer burns. Pick up the leeks, place on the grill and position them on the charcoal-free side. Close the lid and roast using indirect heat for 20–30 minutes until the leeks are soft all the way through. You can measure the core temperature – it should preferably be above 95°C (200°F).

3 Re-heat the broth, add the beans and the Smoked Onions and leave to simmer for a while. Cut the leeks in half and make an incision lengthways on each half. Fill with the beans and broth and garnish with a few fennel flowers.

CHARCOAL-ROASTED RED BEETROOT
with feta and dukkah

Serves 6

6 small red beetroot (beets)

6 slices of sourdough bread

unsalted butter

60 g (2 oz) feta, preferably made
    with goat's milk

6 teaspoons Dukkah, see recipe on p. 168

fresh mixed herbs, e.g. oregano, parsley, shiso
    leaves and basil

sea salt flakes

1 Add charcoal or firewood to half the barbecue (grill) so that you have space to roast the beetroot using indirect heat later. Light the barbecue and once it is burning strongly, place the beetroots straight onto the charcoal so that the outer layer burns. Turn several times using tongs. Pick up the beetroots, place on the grill and position them on the charcoal-free side. Close the lid and roast using indirect heat for around 1 hour until the beetroots feel soft when you gently press the skin. You can measure the core temperature – it should preferably be above 85°C (185°F).

2 Peel the beetroots once they are cool enough to handle without burning yourself. It can be a little tricky to remove the skin – try pulling it off with your fingers; otherwise, cut it off with a knife.

3 Let the barbecue get really hot so you can toast the bread. Butter the slices of bread. First, grill them quickly on the side without butter, then turn them over onto the buttered side and grill them until there are clear grill stripes.

4 Slice the beetroot and crumble some feta on top. Place them on the grill briefly so that the cheese begins to melt.

5 Place a few slices of beetroot with feta onto each slice of toast, sprinkle some Dukkah over them and top with herbs and sea salt flakes.

CHARCOAL-ROASTED SWEET POTATO
with creamed white beans

Serves 6

6 medium sweet potatoes

Creamed white beans with goat's cheese

2 tablespoons unsalted butter

40 g (1½ oz) finely chopped shallots

1 tablespoon finely chopped garlic

1 tablespoon white wine vinegar

600 g (1 lb 5 oz/3 cups) large white beans, cooked

1 teaspoon finely grated unwaxed lemon zest

200 ml (7 fl oz/scant 1 cup) Vegetable Stock, see
    recipe on p. 162

200 ml (7 fl oz/scant 1 cup) double (heavy) cream

100 g (3½ oz) soft goat's cheese (chèvre)

To serve

parsley leaves

olive oil

sea salt flakes and black pepper

1. Light the barbecue (grill). Pierce the sweet potatoes in a few places using a cocktail stick (toothpick) then place them straight onto the glowing charcoal. This can even be done while the charcoal is still burning. Roast the sweet potatoes until the skin has charred completely and they are soft inside, around 20 minutes.

2. Dollop the butter into a saucepan and put on a medium heat. Add the shallots and garlic and fry until soft without taking on any colour. Add the vinegar and stir a few times. Add the beans and lemon zest and continue to stir until everything is thoroughly combined. Add the Vegetable Stock, cream and goat's cheese, reduce the heat slightly and leave to simmer on a low heat until the cheese has completely melted.

3. Cut a lengthways incision into the sweet potatoes. Hollow them out, trying to keep as much of the brown flesh inside the skin as possible without taking too much of the charred skin. Set aside.

4. Pour the creamy beans into bowls, generously spoon sweet potatoes over these and top with parsley, olive oil, salt and pepper.

EXPEDITIONARY STORES **This is one of the dishes I love to take out into the woods with me. Fill a vacuum flask with the creamy beans and bring a raw sweet potato for the camp fire.**

LEVE'S PIZZA DOUGH

Makes 6 pizzas

1 kg (2 lb 4 oz/8 cups) strong flour
700 ml (24 fl oz/scant 3 cups) + 70 ml (2½ fl oz/
    5 tablespoons) water at 40°C (100°F)
200 g (7 oz) active sourdough starter
4 teaspoons sea salt flakes

1 Mix the flour, 700 ml (24 fl oz/scant 3 cups) of
   water and the sourdough by hand in a mixing
   bowl until the temperature of the dough falls
   to 30–33°C (86–91°F). Cover in cling film
   (plastic wrap) and leave to rest for 30 minutes. Add the salt and knead it into the dough
   together with 70 ml (2½ fl oz/5 tablespoons)
   of water. Leave the dough to prove at room
   temperature for 1 hour. Fold the dough once
   every 20 minutes while proving: moisten your
   hand and pick up the dough's outer edge, pull it
   carefully and fold it towards the middle. Continue until you have gone all the way around.

2 Leave the dough in the refrigerator for
   24 hours. During that time, the dough should
   increase in volume by 30–50 per cent and
   feel airy, bubbly and lively. Place the dough
   on a floured baking board. Divide into pieces
   of around 300 g (10½ oz). Shape the pieces
   of dough into small balls, but take care not to
   press too much air out of them. Sprinkle a little flour on each ball, cover them with a dish
   towel and then cover in cling film (plastic
   wrap). Leave them to prove at room temperature for 1–2 hours.

3 When the dough balls have finished proving,
   they should have slackened, sunk and in-
   creased in size by around 20 per cent. If you
   carefully push a finger into the dough and
   leave a small mark, the dough is ready to be
   made into pizzas.

A wood oven is a very special way to bake things like pizzas and flatbreads. It is also great for roasting vegetables quickly to give them a crispy edge – for example, the Jerusalem artichokes on p. 139. These days, you can get hold of amazing small wood ovens with a stone base that reaches the perfect heat and can easily climb over 400°C (800°F).

PIZZA with asparagus, pimientos de Padrón, roasted buckwheat and dill oil

Serves 6

6 balls of Pizza Dough, see recipe on p. 120
6 small silver onions, chopped
3 tablespoons rapeseed (canola) oil
100 ml (3½ fl oz/scant ½ cup) white wine
30 asparagus spears
6 tablespoons crème fraîche
180 g (6½ oz) mozzarella
6 mild green chillies, e.g. pimientos de Padrón,
    finely sliced

To serve

olive oil
6 tablespoons Roasted Buckwheat, see recipe
    on p.170

1. Heat the wood oven to the highest temperature possible – 350–400°C (660–800°F) is perfect. Leave for a while to ensure that the stone is really hot.
2. Place the onions in a cold saucepan. Add the rapeseed oil and place the pan on a medium heat. The onions will soon start to release liquid and the flavours will be concentrated through the onions cooking in their own juices. Stir once every 5 minutes for 15–20 minutes. Take care to ensure that the onions don't take on colour or burn to the bottom of the pan. Add the wine and reduce for around 15 minutes until almost all the liquid is gone. Set aside and leave to cool.
3. Cut the tops off the asparagus spears and cut the rest into slices around 5 mm (¼ in) thick.
4. Dust a large chopping board generously with flour. Take a ball of Pizza Dough, shape it into a round pizza and leave it to rest for a few minutes. Dust the pizza paddle with flour and place the pizza base on the paddle while pulling gently at the edges to stretch it out further.
5. Take 1 tablespoon of crème fraîche and spread it out from the middle of the pizza base towards the edge in a thin layer. Tear the mozzarella and place small pieces across the pizza, around 30 g (1 oz) per pizza.
6. Add a thin layer of onions, asparagus and Padrón peppers, and put the pizza in the oven. Once the edges of the pizza have bubbled up and taken on a good colour – preferably a little burnt in places – it is ready. Remove the pizza from the oven and brush the crusts with olive oil and top with Roasted Buckwheat.

PIZZA with sweet potato, yellow tomato sauce and Belper Knolle

Serves 6

6 balls of Pizza Dough, see recipe on p. 120

1 sweet potato

1 garlic clove

3 tablespoons unsalted butter, melted

6 tablespoons crème fraîche

2 burrata (weighing 240 g/9 oz)

To serve

marjoram

200 ml (7 fl oz/scant 1 cup) Fermented Yellow Tomato Sauce, see recipe on p. 164

sea salt flakes

Belper Knolle or another hard cheese such as Parmesan

1 Heat the wood oven to the highest temperature possible – 350–400°C (660–800°F) is perfect. Leave for a while to ensure that the stone is really hot.

2 Brush and wash the sweet potato. Dry it carefully and cut it as thinly as possible into slices 1–2 mm (1/16 in) thick – use a mandolin if possible. Place the slices into a bowl, grate the garlic clove over them, add the melted butter and massage it in using your hands.

3 Dust a large chopping board generously with flour. Take a ball of Pizza Dough, shape it into a round pizza and leave it to rest for a few minutes. Dust the pizza paddle with flour and place the pizza base on the paddle while pulling gently at the edges to stretch it out further.

4 Take 1 tablespoon of crème fraîche and spread it out from the middle of the pizza base towards the edge in a thin layer. Tear the burrata and place small pieces across the pizza, around 40 g (1½ oz) per pizza.

5 Add the slices of sweet potato (save the garlic butter) and put the pizza in the oven. Once the edges of the pizza have bubbled up and taken on a good colour – preferably a little burnt in places – it is ready. Remove the pizza from the oven and brush the crusts with garlic butter, then top with marjoram, 2 or 3 tablespoons of the Fermented Yellow Tomato Sauce, salt and shavings of Belper Knolle.

PIZZA with figs, hazelnuts and black garlic dressing

Serves 6

6 balls of Pizza Dough, see recipe on p. 120
6 figs
180 g (6½ oz) hazelnuts (filberts)
6 tablespoons crème fraîche
240 g (8 oz) soft goat's cheese (chèvre)

Dressing
1 vanilla pod (bean)
2 black garlic cloves
4 tablespoons olive oil
2 tablespoons apple cider vinegar
1 tablespoon honey
sea salt flakes

To serve
olive oil

1 Start with the dressing. Cut the vanilla pod lengthways and scrape out the seeds. Place the vanilla seeds together with the other ingredients in a bowl and blend using a hand-held blender or food processor. Set aside.

2 Heat the wood oven to the highest temperature possible – 350–400°C (660–800°F) is perfect. Leave for a while to ensure that the stone is really hot.

3 Cut the figs into thin slices, around 3–4 mm (⅛ in) thick. Halve the hazelnuts.

4 Dust a large chopping board generously with flour. Take a ball of Pizza Dough, shape it into a round pizza and leave it to rest for a few minutes. Dust the pizza paddle with flour and place the pizza base on the paddle while pulling gently at the edges to stretch it out further.

5 Take 1 tablespoon of crème fraîche and spread it out from the middle of the pizza base towards the edge in a thin layer. Place small chunks of goat's cheese on top, around 40 g (1½ oz) per pizza.

6 Add the fig slices and hazelnuts and put the pizza in the oven. Once the edges of the pizza have bubbled up and taken on a good colour – preferably a little burnt in places – it is ready. Remove from the oven and brush the crusts with olive oil and drizzle a tablespoon of dressing on top.

131

PIZZA with pumpkin and chanterelles

Serves 6

6 balls of Pizza Dough, see recipe on p. 120
1 small Uchiki Kuri pumpkin (winter squash) or
    butternut squash
1 garlic clove
2 tablespoons olive oil
6 tablespoons crème fraîche
240 g (8 oz) soft goat's cheese (chèvre)
180 g (6 oz) chanterelle mushrooms

To serve
oregano leaves
oxalis (wood sorrel) (preferably with flowers)
sea salt flakes

1 Heat the wood oven to the highest temperature possible – 350–400°C (660–800°F) is perfect. Leave for a while to ensure that the stone is really hot.

2 Peel the squash and cut into thin slices, preferably using a mandolin. Place the slices into a bowl, grate the garlic over them, add the oil and massage it in using your hands.

3 Dust a large chopping board generously with flour. Take a ball of Pizza Dough, shape it into a round pizza and leave it to rest for a few minutes. Dust the pizza paddle with flour and place the pizza base on the paddle while pulling gently at the edges to stretch it out further.

4 Take 1 tablespoon of crème fraîche and spread it out from the middle of the pizza base towards the edge in a thin layer. Place small chunks of goat's cheese on top, around 40 g (1½ oz) per pizza.

5 Add the slices of squash and mushrooms and put the pizza in the oven. Once the edges of the pizza have bubbled up and taken on a good colour – preferably a little burned in places – it is ready. Remove from the oven and brush the crusts with the garlic oil before garnishing with oregano, oxalis and a little salt.

MAXIMISE HEAT **Regardless of whether you have access to a wood oven or a normal oven, the trick is to get it to the highest temperature possible and to use some kind of flat stone to bake the pizza on. I use a wood oven from Ooni that is good value and easy to use. But there are plenty of other ways to bake pizza – including a normal barbecue (grill), so use trial and error to find the best option for you.**

PIZZA with blue potatoes, Brussels sprouts and truffle

Serves 6

6 balls of Pizza Dough, see recipe on p. 120

6 small blue potatoes

1 garlic clove

3 tablespoons unsalted butter, melted

6 tablespoons crème fraîche

180 g (6½ oz) mozzarella

180 g (6½ oz) pecorino

12 Brussels sprouts

To serve

fresh truffle

1   Heat the wood oven to the highest temperature possible – 350–400°C (660–800°F) is perfect. Leave for a while to ensure that the stone is really hot.

2   Brush and wash the potatoes. Dry them carefully and cut them as thinly as possible into slices 1–2 mm (¹⁄₁₆ in) thick – use a mandolin if possible. Place the slices into a bowl, grate the garlic over them, add the melted butter and massage it in using your hands.

3   Dust a large chopping board generously with flour. Take a ball of Pizza Dough, shape it into a round pizza and leave it to rest for a few minutes. Dust the pizza paddle with flour and place the pizza base on the paddle while pulling gently at the edges to stretch it out further.

4   Take 1 tablespoon of crème fraîche and spread it out from the middle of the pizza base towards the edge in a thin layer. Tear the mozzarella and place small pieces across the pizza, around 30 g (1 oz) per pizza. Crumble the pecorino into small pieces and spread across the pizza, around 30 g (1 oz) on each.

5   Add the slices of potato, finely slice the Brussels sprouts and sprinkle on top, then put the pizza in the oven. Once the edges of the pizza had bubbled up and taken on a good colour – preferably a little burnt in places – it is ready. Remove the pizza from the oven and brush the crusts with the garlic butter and garnish with shavings of truffle.

FLATBREAD with carrots and sage

Serves 6

300 ml (10 fl oz/1¼ cups) kefir (or filmjölk)

2 teaspoons dried yeast

1 egg

2 tablespoons rapeseed (canola) oil

1 tablespoon honey

1 teaspoon salt

400 g (14 oz/3¼ cups) plain (all-purpose) flour

½ teaspoon baking powder

Topping

2 purple carrots

2 yellow carrots

2 garlic cloves

3 tablespoons ghee or melted unsalted butter

sage leaves

sea salt flakes

1 Take the kefir out of the refrigerator well in advance so that it is close to room temperature. Place the dried yeast in a mixing bowl and whisk in the kefir so that the yeast dissolves. Add the egg, oil, honey and salt and whisk until smooth.

2 Mix together the flour and baking powder in a bowl. Gradually add it a little at a time to the kefir and knead into a smooth dough for 7 minutes using a dough hook. The dough should come away from the edges of the bowl and not stick. The quantity of flour can vary, so make sure you have a little extra on hand.

3 Cover the dough with a dish towel. Leave to prove for 1–1½ hours, or until the dough has doubled in size.

4 Divide the dough into six pieces and shape into round balls by folding in the edges towards the middle so that you have a nice surface tension.

Place the balls on a floured baking sheet with the joint facing down and press them gently with the palm of your hand. Cover with a dish towel and leave them to prove for another hour.

5 Heat the oven to the highest temperature possible – 350–400°C (660–800°F) is perfect. Leave for a while to ensure that the stone is really hot.

6 Dust a large chopping board generously with flour. Take a dough ball and flatten it into a circle. Work it with a rolling pin in one direction so that the bread becomes an oval shape and leave the dough to rest for a few minutes. Dust the pizza paddle with flour and place the flatbread on the paddle while pulling gently at the edges to make it slightly more taut.

7 Cut the carrots lengthways into thin slices. Grate the garlic into the ghee and brush over the bread. Distribute the carrot slices and sage leaves evenly across the bread. Brush again with the garlic ghee and top with a little sea salt flakes.

8 Put in the oven and bake for around 1½ minutes or until the edges take on a lovely, golden yellow, somewhat burnt tone.

135

WOOD OVEN ROASTED CARROTS
with labneh

Serves 6

1 litre (34 fl oz/4 cups) plain yoghurt

12 medium purple carrots

100 ml (3½ fl oz/scant ½ cup) apple brandy,
 e.g. calvados

1 tablespoon honey

2 tablespoons rapeseed (canola) oil

sea salt flakes

1 Put a funnel with a coffee filter paper in it in a jug and pour in the yoghurt. Leave in the refrigerator for 24 hours. When you take it out, you should have around half a litre of whey in the jug and a thick, creamy labneh in the filter paper.

2 Light your wood oven or set your oven to its highest temperature, around 230°C (450°F/gas 10).

3 Soak the carrots for a while to remove most of the soil and gravel. Remove them from the water and scrub them gently with a root vegetable brush to remove anything else. Use a small vegetable knife to scrape around the base of the leaves so that you remove all the soil bacteria.

Dry the carrots carefully with a dish towel and set to one side.

4 Put a frying pan (skillet) on a medium heat. Pour in the yoghurt whey and bring to the boil. Add the carrots and cook them for 10–15 minutes until they are soft on the outside.

5 Remove the carrots, but let the whey continue to cook in the pan. Let the carrots steam until dry and then put them in a baking tray (pan).

6 Pour the apple brandy and honey into the whey. Raise the heat slightly and cook until it has reduced to one sixth of the volume while stirring constantly, this will take around 15–20 minutes. Remove from the heat and set to one side.

7 Drizzle the rapeseed oil and sprinkle the sea salt flakes over the carrots and then put them in the wood oven. Remove them after 1–2 minutes, shake the baking tray and then return it to the oven. Repeat this four times. Remove the carrots from the oven and then leave to rest.

8 Put a large spoonful of labneh and two carrots onto each plate. Drizzle a couple of spoonfuls of the whey reduction on top.

JERUSALEM ARTICHOKE SOUP
made with smoked buttermilk

Serves 6

600 g (1 lb 5 oz) Jerusalem artichokes

6–7 garlic cloves, crushed with the skin on

1 sprig of thyme

1 sprig of oregano

3 tablespoons rapeseed (canola) oil

sea salt flakes

Soup base

1 tablespoon Smoked Butter, see recipe on p. 149

1 tablespoon rapeseed (canola) oil

70 g (2½ oz) finely chopped shallots

400 ml (13 fl oz/generous 1½ cups) dry apple cider

200 ml (7 fl oz/scant 1 cup) Vegetable Stock, see
recipe on p. 162

400 ml (13 fl oz/generous 1½ cups) Smoked
Buttermilk, see recipe on p. 149

To serve

6 tablespoons melted Smoked Butter, see recipe for
Smoked Butter on p. 149

watercress

sea salt flakes and black pepper

1. Light the wood oven and let it reach a temperature of around 250°C (480°F).
2. Wash and scrub the Jerusalem artichokes thoroughly. Dry them completely using a dish towel and then put them on a baking sheet together with the garlic and herbs. Drizzle with rapeseed oil and sprinkle some sea salt flakes on top before putting the sheet in the oven. Remove it after 4–5 minutes, shake the baking sheet and then return it to the oven. Repeat this four times. Remove the baking sheet and cover with kitchen foil so that the artichokes continue to steam and cook in their own heat. Leave them to stand for 10–15 minutes. Cut one third of the Jerusalem artichokes into slices 5 mm (¼ in) thick and set aside. Hollow out the rest and use for the stock. You should be left with 300 g (10 ½ oz) flesh from the Jerusalem artichokes.
3. Mix the Smoked Butter and oil in a cold saucepan. Add the shallots and then put the saucepan on a medium heat. Stir constantly using a wooden spoon and let the shallots soften without taking on any colour, around 10 minutes. Pour over the apple cider, raise the heat and leave to cook for another 5 minutes. Add the Vegetable Stock, Smoked Buttermilk and Jerusalem artichokes. Reduce the heat, whisk thoroughly so that everything is properly mixed and then leave to simmer for a further 10 minutes. Remove from the heat, cover with a lid and set aside.
4. Place a small heap of sliced Jerusalem artichokes in each dish and distribute the soup between the dishes. Drizzle a little melted butter over each bowl and top with watercress, salt and pepper.

WOOD OVEN ROASTED CHESTNUTS
with asparagus and smoked cream

Serves 6

600 g (1 lb 5 oz) asparagus spears
2 tablespoons rapeseed (canola) oil
400 g (14 oz) whole chestnuts
2 tablespoons melted unsalted butter
sea salt flakes

To serve

200 ml (7 fl oz/scant 1 cup) Smoked Cream, see
    recipe on p. 149
rind of ½ unwaxed lime
nasturtiums, leaves and flowers, or watercress
sea salt flakes

1 Light the wood oven and let it reach a temperature of around 300°C (575°F).

2 Trim and wash the asparagus spears. Dry them and place them in a bowl together with a tablespoon of oil. Mix so that everything is covered in oil.

3 Score a cross in the top of each chestnut. Put them in a cast-iron pan, drizzle a tablespoon of rapeseed oil over, sprinkle with some sea salt flakes and put them in the wood oven. Remove after 1–2 minutes, shake the pan then return it to the oven. Repeat this four times. Remove the chestnuts from the oven and leave to rest.

4 Place the asparagus in a cast-iron pan and put it in the oven. Remove from the oven after around 1 minute – they cook quickly so keep an eye on them. Shake the pan or turn the asparagus over and return to the oven for another minute. Once done, remove the asparagus and set aside.

5 Peel the chestnuts and put them in a bowl with the melted butter and stir. Remove the chestnuts after a few minutes and set aside. Pour the Smoked Cream into the bowl and grate the lime rind over the top. Whisk so that the cream and butter combine.

6 Pour 2–3 tablespoons of Smoked Cream onto each plate and place the chestnuts and asparagus on top. Garnish with the nasturtiums and a pinch of salt.

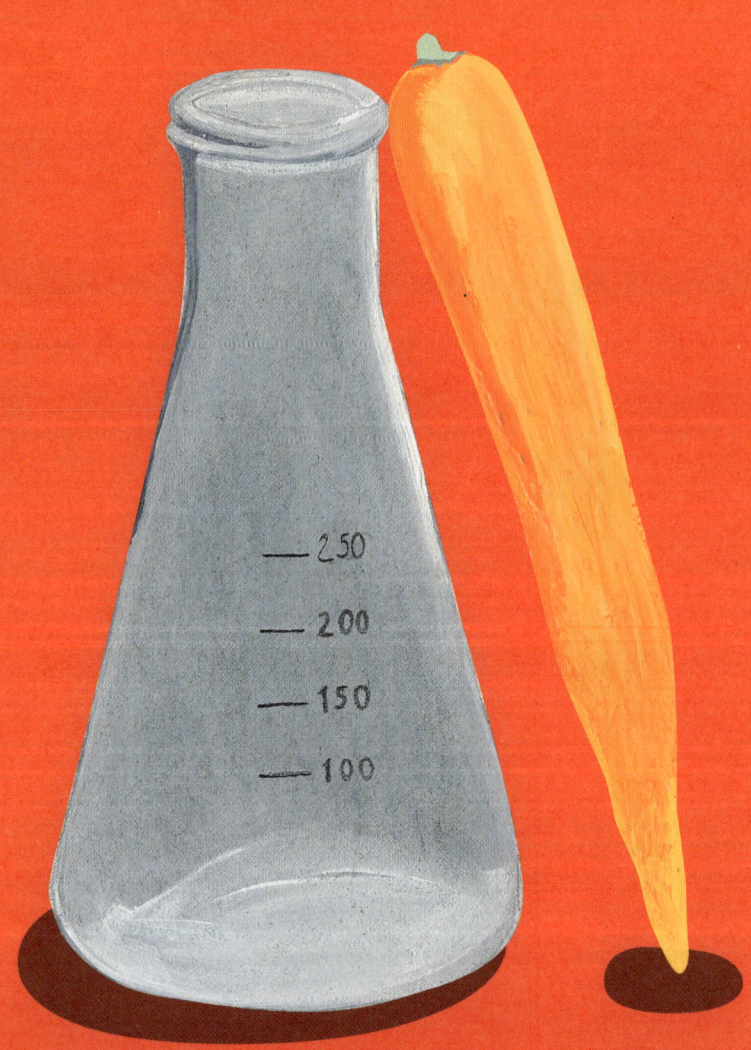

SMOKED CREAM

700 ml (24 fl oz/scant 3 cups) double (heavy) cream
glowing charcoal

1 Light the barbecue (grill) with wood so that there is a strong glow.
2 Pour the cream into a heatproof container. Select a glowing piece of charcoal by eye and pick it up with tongs. Put the charcoal in the cream and leave it there for a few hours, preferably overnight in the refrigerator.
3 Strain through a coarse meshed strainer.

SMOKED BUTTER AND BUTTERMILK

700 ml (24 fl oz/scant 3 cups) Smoked Cream, see
    adjacent recipe
sea salt flakes

1 Whisk the cream until it turns to butter. How long this takes depends on which method you use, but you will be able to clearly tell when it is ready. The liquid that gathers around the lump of butter is the buttermilk – keep it, because it is great for cooking with vegetables and legumes.
2 Rinse the lump of butter under cold water and let the last of the liquid drain. Put the butter in a dish towel and dry it carefully, ensuring you remove the liquid on the surface. Salt thoroughly, store in an airtight container and put in the refrigerator.

PLANT-BASED SMOKING **Naturally, you can use the same techniques for smoking nut- and oat-based alternatives.**

COLD SOUR TOMATO SOUP

Serves 6

1.5 litres (50 fl oz/6 cups) Fermented Yellow Tomato
    Sauce, see recipe on p. 164
360 ml (12 fl oz/1½ cups) gin (60 ml/2 fl oz/
    ¼ cup per portion)
a few drops of habanero sauce (optional)

Kohlrabi in elderflower vinegar

2 small kohlrabi
100 ml (3½ fl oz/scant ½ cup) elderflower vinegar,
    alternatively Champagne vinegar or apple cider
    vinegar
small pinch of sea salt flakes

To serve

Smoked Tomatoes + a little of the oil, see recipe on
    p. 172
multigrain crackers
elderflowers (optional)

1 Peel and dice the kohlrabi into bite-sized pieces. Put the cubes of kohlrabi in a bowl then add the vinegar and salt and leave to soak for around 1 hour.

2 Thoroughly mix the Fermented Yellow Tomato Sauce with the gin and habanero sauce in a large jug.

3 Pour around 300 ml (10 fl oz/1¼ cups) of soup into each bowl, add 3–4 Smoked Tomatoes and drizzle a little of the smoked oil on top. Finish with 2 tablespoons of kohlrabi cubes, multigrain crackers and elderflowers, if they are in season.

COLDER SOUP **Personally, I like my soup at refrigerator temperature, but you can also add a few ice cubes if you would like an even more cooling dish on a hot summer's day.**

Saw a deep cross into a big piece of wood as this can function as a hearth and grill. Ignite some sawdust in the bottom of the cross and let it burn along the piece of wood until you have a nice glow. It will burn for several hours.

SMOKY ONION SOUP with white mould cheese gratin

Serves 6

12 medium yellow onions, finely chopped

4 tablespoons unsalted butter

1 tablespoon white wine vinegar

1 teaspoon salt

500 ml (17 fl oz/2 cups) white wine

500 ml (17 fl oz/2 cups) Vegetable Stock,
　　see recipe on p. 162

Baked white mould cheese

1 white mould cheese, e.g. brie, preferably
　　in a wooden box

1 garlic clove, quartered

1 sprig of rosemary

2 tablespoons white wine

To serve

toasted bread

thyme leaves

1　Set fire to a few pieces of firewood in a barbecue (grill) with a lid then place the grill on top, or set fire to sawdust in a large, sawn piece of wood (see p. 153).

2　Mix the onions, butter, vinegar and salt in a cold, wet terrine dish. Place over the flames and cover with a lid. The onions will soon start to release liquid and the flavours will be concentrated through the onions cooking in their own juices. Stir using a wooden spoon every 15 minutes to 1 hour. Take care to make sure it does not burn. (If you notice that it is getting too dry, you can add the wine a little earlier.) Every time you stir it, circle the lid above the terrine so that the smoke seeps into the pot and flavours the onions.

3　Pour in the wine and Vegetable Stock after about 1 hour and leave to simmer for a further 2–3 hours, depending on temperature. The onions should be a dark brown colour and the liquid should have reduced by at least a quarter. Check the terrine occasionally and circle the lid to add more smoke.

4　Remove from the heat and add new charcoal or wood to one side of the barbecue and light. If you have a barbecue thermometer, the temperature should be around 200°C (400°F). Put the cheese in its wooden box in a baking tray (it may leak slightly so it's good to have a container to catch this). Score a cross in the cheese and insert the garlic. Add a small sprig of rosemary and pour the wine over. Put the baking tray on the grill, close the lid and let it bake using indirect heat for around 20 minutes. At the same time, toast the bread on the grill above the glowing charcoal.

5　Serve the onion soup topped with some thyme alongside the cheese in its tray. Dip the toast in the cheese and spoon onions on top. Open wide and let those onions make you cry.

ENSURE SUCCESS WITH ONIONS **When I cut up onions to cook them for a long time, I want the pieces to be as even as possible. I start by cutting off the root and top of the onion before halving them lengthways from root to top. Then I peel the onion and continue to cut in the same direction into pieces as evenly sized as possible, around 3–4 mm (⅙ in) thick.**

SMOKY BEETROOT AND MUSHROOM STEW

Serves 6

3 red beetroot (beets)

3 yellow beetroot (beets)

2 tablespoons rapeseed (canola) oil

300 g (10½ oz) mixed mushrooms, cut into generous
    pieces

3 yellow onions, peeled and quartered

2 garlic cloves, crushed with the skin on

1 bay leaf

1 sprig of thyme

1 tablespoon red wine vinegar

600 ml (20 fl oz/2½ cups) red wine

400 ml (13 fl oz/generous 1½ cups) Vegetable
    Stock, see recipe on p. 162

To serve

thyme leaves

parsley leaves

1 tablespoon rapeseed (canola) oil, preferably
    flavoured with thyme

sea salt flakes and black pepper

Quick-pickled Baby Onions, see recipe on p. 175

1 Add charcoal or firewood to half the barbecue (grill) so that you have space to roast the beetroots using indirect heat later. Light the barbecue and once it is burning strongly, place the beetroots straight onto the charcoal so that the outer layer burns. Turn several times using tongs. Place the grill on high and position the beetroots away from the flames. Close the lid and roast using indirect heat for 1 hour until the beetroots feel soft when you gently press the skin. You can measure the core temperature – it should be above 90°C (195°F). Remove from the grill and leave to cool.

2 Continue with the next step while the beetroots are roasting. Set fire to a few pieces of firewood in a barbecue with a lid and then place the grill on top, or set fire to sawdust in a large, sawn piece of wood (see p. 153).

3 Pour oil into a wet terrine dish and position above the flames. Add the mushrooms when the oil begins to smoke and let them take on colour, stirring occasionally. Remove using a slotted spoon and set aside.

4 Put the onions into the oil and fry until they begin to soften and take on colour, around 5 minutes. Add the garlic cloves, bay leaf and thyme and stir a few times. Add the vinegar and wait for 1 minute for it to be fried off and absorbed by the onions, stirring constantly to stop it from burning. Pour in the wine and Vegetable Stock and leave to simmer for another 1 hour. Check the liquid occasionally to ensure it is not boiling away, stirring when you do. When opening the lid, circle it above the terrine so that the smoke seeps into the pot and flavours it. Strain the stock into another container and clean the terrine.

5 Peel the beetroots once they have cooled slightly. Try pulling the skin off using your fingers, otherwise cut it off using a knife. Cut the beetroots into generous pieces that can be eaten using a spoon.

6 Place the terrine back over the glowing charcoal, add the mushrooms and beetroots. Pour the stock over. Bring the pot back to the boil. Remove from the heat and tear in some thyme and parsley. Top with the oil and season with salt and pepper to taste. Serve alongside a bowl of the Quick-pickled Baby Onions.

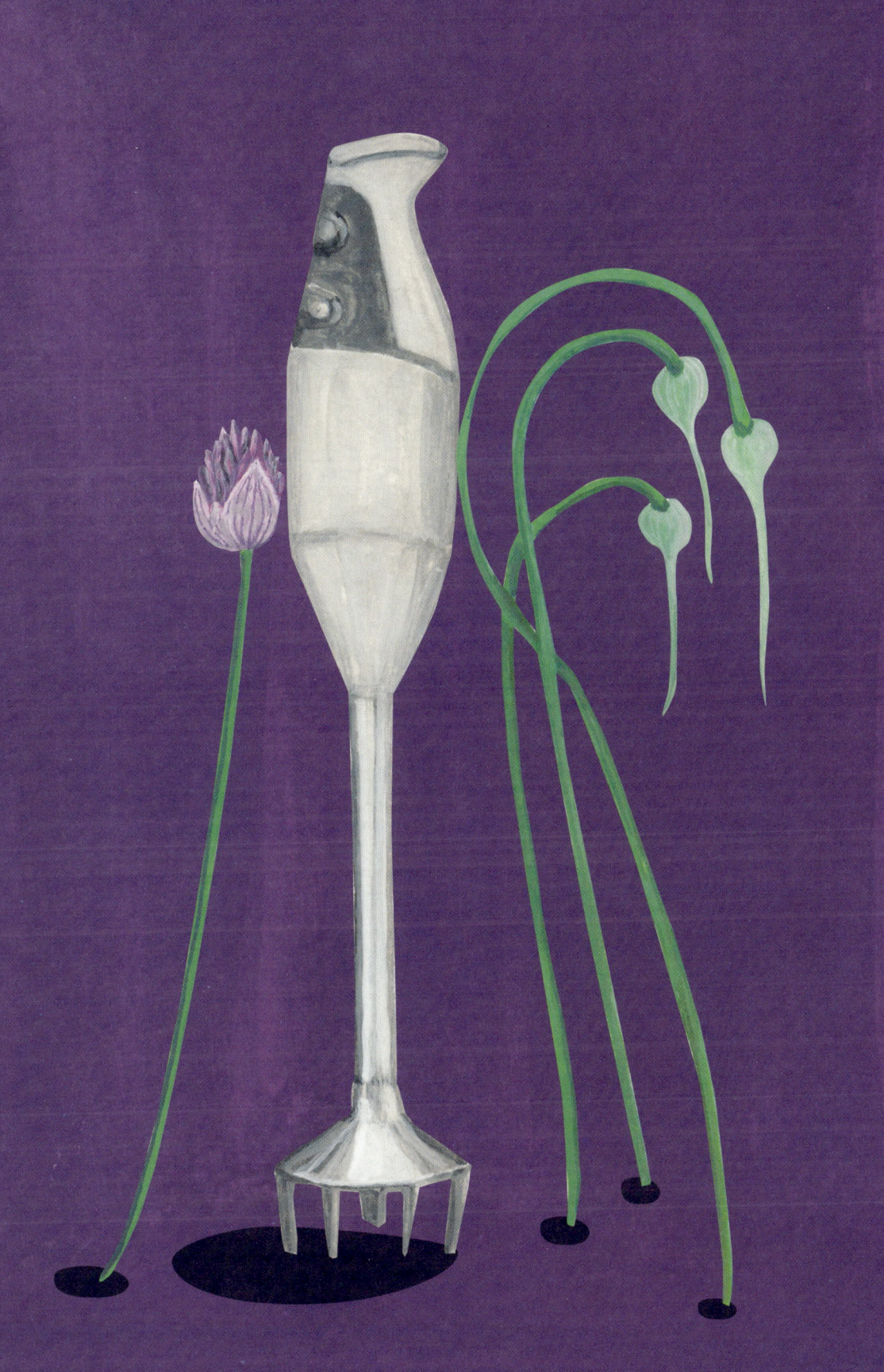

VEGETABLE STOCK

Makes about 2 litres (68 fl oz/8 cups)

2 tablespoons rapeseed (canola) oil

140 g (5 oz) coarsely chopped yellow onion

80 g (3 oz) coarsely chopped leek

50 g (2 oz) coarsely chopped carrot

100 g (3½ oz) coarsely chopped celery stalks

40 g (1½ oz) coarsely chopped fennel

1 whole garlic, halved and crushed

2 bay leaves

1 teaspoon white peppercorns

1 teaspoon coriander seeds

1 tablespoon white wine vinegar

4 litres (140 fl oz/16 cups) water

6 sprigs of parsley

4 sprigs of lovage

1. Pour the oil into a large saucepan and put on a medium heat. Add all the ingredients except the water, parsley and lovage and stir until everything is thoroughly mixed. Fry until the vegetables soften, this usually takes 5–7 minutes. Stir occasionally so that the vegetables do not take on too much colour.

2. Raise the heat, add the water and cook until the stock has been reduced in volume by around half, around 1–1½ hours.

3. Remove the pan from the heat. Add the parsley and lovage and leave covered for another 20–30 minutes. Strain the stock into a mixing bowl and keep in the refrigerator or pour into an ice cube tray and freeze.

PICKLED RED ONIONS

salt

500 g (1 lb 2 oz) red onions, finely sliced

Spicy 1–2–3 syrup

200 ml (7 fl oz/scant 1 cup) vinegar, preferably 12 per cent

330 g (11 fl oz/1⅔ cups) caster (superfine) sugar or cane sugar

600 ml (20 fl oz/2½ cups) water

3 coriander roots, finely chopped

2–4 bird's eye chillies

2 bay leaves

1 teaspoon black peppercorns

1 teaspoon coriander seeds

1 teaspoon pink peppercorns

1. Start with the syrup. Boil the vinegar, sugar and water, then stir until the sugar has dissolved. Add the herbs and spices, reduce the heat and leave to simmer for a few minutes. Strain the syrup and leave to cool – ideally leave in the refrigerator so that cools completely.

2. Boil a pan of water with plenty of salt. Add the onions and blanch for around 2 minutes. Pour the onions into a colander and rinse with cold water until they are cold. Place the onions in a mixing bowl with cold water and ice cubes.

3. Drain the onions and put in a glass jar. Pour the syrup in and put the jar in the refrigerator. The pickled onions will be ready after 24 hours.

FERMENTED YELLOW TOMATO SAUCE

1 kg (2 lb 4 oz) yellow tomatoes

100 g (3½ oz) celery stalks

24 g (5 teaspoons) salt, without iodine

200 ml (7 fl oz) white kimchi base,
    see adjacent recipe

1 large (1.5 litres/50 fl oz/6 cups) sterilised clip-
    top preserving jar with a rubber seal (such as
    a Kilner jar)

1 Rinse the tomatoes and halve them. Clean the celery and slice it thinly. Put the tomatoes and celery in a bowl and massage in the salt. Apply plenty of pressure to the tomatoes so that they release liquid. Leave to stand at room temperature for at least 1 hour. Stir and apply pressure occasionally.

2 Pour the kimchi base into the bowl and mix using your hands.

3 Pour the mixture into the preserving jar, but leave 2–3 cm (1 in) of air at the top. Fill a plastic bag with some water, knot the bag and add it on top as a weight. Close the lid and seal with the bracket. Place the jar on a plate and ideally stand it in a plastic bag since it is very likely that some liquid will be ejected (make sure you don't seal the bag at the top). Leave the jar to stand at room temperature for 5–7 days.

4 Put the jar in the refrigerator. Remove the jar after a few days, pour it into a bowl and blend until smooth. Strain the sauce and pour into sterilised bottles. Keep in the refrigerator.

WHITE KIMCHI BASE

500 ml (17 fl oz/2 cups) water

2 tablespoons rice flour

100 g (3½ oz) light miso paste

4 shallots, coarsely chopped

2 white or yellow medium carrots, coarsely chopped

100 g (3½ oz) coarsely chopped radishes (around
    3–4 mm)

about 12 g (½ oz) fresh ginger root

50 g (2 oz) coarsely chopped garlic

2 mild white chillies, about 50 g (2 oz),
    e.g. aji pepper

1 Pour the water and rice flour into a saucepan and bring to the boil. Stir constantly to ensure there are no lumps. Reduce the heat and add the miso paste. Stir in and leave to simmer for around 5 minutes. Remove the saucepan from the heat and allow to cool. You can leave the mixture in the refrigerator overnight.

2 Add the shallots, carrots, radishes, ginger and garlic to a food processor and mix into a fine purée. If it is stiff you can add a little splash of water.

3 Pour the rice flour mixture, the vegetable purée and chillies into a glass jar and mix thoroughly. Keep in the refrigerator. If you don't intend to use it for a while, you can also freeze it.

MAYONNAISE USING AQUAFABA

100 ml (3½ fl oz/scant ½ cup) aquafaba (water
    from soaking chickpeas)
1 tablespoon Dijon mustard
1 tablespoon freshly squeezed lemon juice
500 ml (17 fl oz/2 cups) rapeseed (canola) oil
    (not cold pressed)
salt

1 Put all the ingredients except the oil in a beaker or a tall, narrow bowl. Mix using a hand-held blender until everything is blended.

2 Put the hand-held blender touching the bottom of the bowl and add the oil in a thin stream while mixing (hold the hand-held blender still at the bottom of the bowl). When you notice the mayonnaise starting to settle, pull the hand-held blender upwards. Continue mixing to a good consistency and season with salt.

MAYONNAISE USING BOILED POTATOES

2 large potatoes, boiled and peeled (about 300 g/
    10½ oz)
2 tablespoons Dijon mustard
1 teaspoon freshly squeezed lemon juice
1 teaspoon salt
1 pinch of white pepper

Put all the ingredients in a mixer and mix at full power for around 1½ minutes.

MAYONNAISE USING EGGS

2 eggs
1 tablespoon Dijon mustard
1 tablespoon white wine vinegar
2 tablespoons cold-pressed olive oil (optional)
500 ml (17 fl oz/2 cups) rapeseed (canola) oil
    (not cold pressed)
sea salt flakes

1 Crack the eggs into a beaker or a tall, narrow bowl. Add the Dijon mustard, vinegar and olive oil (optional) to add extra flavour. Only using cold-pressed olive oil in the mayonnaise will make it too bitter – a dash, however, will add some sweetness, especially if the mayonnaise is otherwise natural.

2 Mix using a hand-held blender until everything is blended. Put the hand-held blender touching the bottom of the bowl and add the rapeseed oil in a thin stream while mixing (hold the hand-held blender still at the bottom of the bowl). When you notice the mayonnaise starting to settle, pull the hand-held blender upwards. Continue mixing to a good consistency and season with salt.

SRIRACHA MAYONNAISE **Choose one of the basic recipes above and add 2 tablespoons of sriracha sauce once you have mixed it together. Stir in gently.**

DUKKAH

60 g (2 oz) hazelnuts (filberts), without shells

8 macadamia nuts

1 teaspoon coriander seeds

½ teaspoon cumin seeds

1 teaspoon mild chilli powder, e.g. piment d'Espelette

½ teaspoon dried oregano

1 teaspoon salt

1   Put a dry frying pan (skillet) on a medium heat and add the nuts and coriander seeds. Roast for about 5 minutes until golden-brown. Stir occasionally to ensure they do not burn. Take off the heat.

2   Place in a food processor and add the cumin, chilli, oregano and salt. Run a few blitzes or pulses – it should be in small pieces but not too finely chopped. Store in a dry, airtight container.

CHICORY DUKKAH

3 tablespoons sweet almonds

8 walnuts

1 tablespoon sunflower seeds

1 tablespoon white sesame seeds

1 teaspoon coriander seeds

1 teaspoon nigella seeds

1 teaspoon dried chicory (endive) root

1 teaspoon salt

1   Put a dry frying pan (skillet) on a medium heat and add the nuts, sunflower, sesame and coriander seeds. Roast for about 5 minutes until golden-brown. Stir occasionally to ensure it does not burn. Take off the heat.

2   Place in a food processor and add the nigella seeds, chicory and salt. Run a few blitzes or pulses – it should be in small pieces but not too finely chopped. Store in a dry, airtight container.

BLACK DUKKAH

1 leek, leaves only

1 slice of dark rye bread (preferably sweetened with malt syrup)

50 g (2 oz) walnuts

1 tablespoon black sesame seeds

1 teaspoon coriander seeds

1 teaspoon nigella seeds

1 tablespoon finely chopped ancho chilli

1 teaspoon black Himalaya salt

1   Set the oven to the highest temperature. Cut the leeks into long, thin, flat strips. Place on a baking sheet and put in the oven for a few minutes until the leeks are completely black. Remove the baking sheet and turn over the leaves. Return to the oven and let the other side turn black. Remove and leave to cool. Use a food processor to blitz the leaves into a fine powder.

2   Put a dry frying pan (skillet) on a medium heat. Tear the bread and add it together with the walnuts, sesame seeds and coriander seeds. Toast until everything takes on a little colour and begins to smell fragrant, around 5 minutes. Stir occasionally to ensure it does not burn. Take off the heat.

3   Put the mixture in a food processor, add the nigella seeds, chilli and salt and run a few blitzes or pulses. It should be in small pieces but not too finely chopped. Store in a dry, airtight container.

FURIKAKE WITH ROASTED BLACK KALE

10 g (½ oz) black kale leaves

2 tablespoons whole buckwheat

2 tablespoons sweet almonds

2 tablespoons sunflower seeds

1 tablespoon black sesame seeds

1 tablespoon white sesame seeds

½ teaspoon Sichuan peppercorns

10 g (½ oz) dried dead man's fingers (or dried nori)

sea salt flakes

1 Set the oven to 120°C (250°F/gas 1). Place the black kale on a baking sheet and roast until completely dry and crispy, around 20 minutes.

2 Put a dry frying pan (skillet) on a medium heat and add the buckwheat, sweet almonds, sunflower seeds, sesame seeds and Sichuan peppercorns. Toast until beginning to colour and smells fragrant, around 5 minutes. Stir occasionally to ensure it does not burn. Take off the heat.

3 Put the nut mixture in a food processor, crumble in the black kale leaves and seaweed and add a pinch of salt. Run a few blitzes or pulses – it should be in small pieces but not too finely chopped. Store the furikake in a dry, airtight container.

ROASTED BUCKWHEAT

280 g (10 oz/1⅔ cups) whole buckwheat

1 tablespoon rapeseed (canola) oil

1 Rinse the buckwheat in hot water and then cold water. Place in a mixing bowl, fill with water and leave to stand for at least 1 hour.

2 Strain and place the buckwheat on a dish towel and let it dry slightly.

3 Put a frying pan (skillet) on a medium heat, add the oil and let it heat up. Add the buckwheat just before the oil begins to smoke. Fry the buckwheat until it turns crispy and golden brown, around 5 minutes. Stir occasionally to ensure it does not burn.

HARISSA

6 mild red chillies

1 large red (bell) pepper

1 teaspoon sea salt flakes

½ teaspoon coriander seeds

½ teaspoon cumin seeds

½ teaspoon black peppercorns

2 tablespoons rapeseed (canola) oil

100 g (3½ oz) finely chopped red onion

3 garlic cloves, finely chopped

1½ tablespoons tomato purée

2 tablespoons freshly squeezed lemon juice

1 teaspoon salt

1   Light the barbecue (grill) and while the fire is still burning grill the chillies and pepper hard so they turn black. Transfer into a plastic bag with the salt and let them steam in their own heat. After 10–15 minutes, when they are cool enough to handle, remove the skin from the chillies and pepper by massaging them while they are still in the bag. Remove them from the bag and cut them lengthways. Remove the seeds but reserve these for the next step. Chop the fruit finely.

2   Heat a cast-iron pan on a medium heat. Toast the reserved chilli and pepper seeds together with the coriander, cumin and black peppercorns until everything turns golden brown and you can clearly smell the spices, around 2 minutes. Crush the spices coarsely using a pestle and mortar.

3   Heat a cast-iron pan on a medium-to-high heat and add the oil. Add the onion and garlic when it begins to smoke and fry for around 5 minutes while stirring. Add the chillies, pepper and tomato purée and leave to simmer for around 10 minutes while stirring. The mixture should be a dark colour and almost caramelised.

4   Transfer into a food processor together with the lemon juice, crushed spices and salt. Blend until smooth. Add a little more oil if it gets too thick. Keep in a sterilised glass jar in the refrigerator. It will keep for at least 2 weeks.

MIDSUMMER'S LOUISIANA HOT SAUCE

500 g (1 lb 2 oz) red jalapeños

1 tablespoon rapeseed (canola) oil

2½ teaspoons sea salt flakes

2½ teaspoons water

100 ml (3½ fl oz/scant ½ cup) Champagne vinegar or white wine vinegar

1   Cut the tops off the jalapeños and remove the core. Set aside 100 g (3½ oz). Put the remaining 400 g (14 oz) in a bowl together with the oil. Then stir to ensure everything is coated.

2   Light the barbecue (grill) and while the fire is still burning grill the jalapeños hard so that the skins turn black. Set aside and leave to cool completely.

3   Place all the chillies, salt and water in a food processor and blend until smooth. Pour into a fermentation jar with a water trap and leave at room temperature for at least 6 weeks.

4   Press the mixture through a sieve (fine-mesh strainer). Add the vinegar and fill sterilised glass bottles. The sauce will keep in the refrigerator for several years.

SMOKIER SAUCE **If you want a little more of the smoky flavour, you can buy a burnt oak infusion spiral (medium strength) that you can put in the jar during step 3 of the fermentation process. They are available to buy from shops that sell brewing and wine making equipment.**

SMOKED ONIONS

500 g (1 lb 2 oz) onions, halved

1 garlic bulb, halved widthways

fresh mixed herbs, e.g. rosemary and thyme

rind of 1 unwaxed lemon

200 ml (7 fl oz/scant 1 cup) rapeseed (canola) oil

½ teaspoon salt

100–200 g (3½–7 oz) smoker chips

1 Light the barbecue (grill). Get a large baking tray and a smaller heatproof plate with a 1–1½ cm (½ in) high edge (the edge cannot be higher than the one on the large baking tray). Place a thin layer of smoker chips in the bottom of the large baking tray then place the smaller plate in the tray.

2 Position the onions with the cut-side facing upwards together with the garlic, herbs and lemon rind on the smaller plate. Drizzle with the oil and sprinkle with the salt. Cover with kitchen foil and place the baking tray with the plate on the grill while there are still flames. After a few minutes, the chips will begin to smoke and the smoke will seep out from under the foil (if the smoke doesn't seep out, you can unfold the foil a little at one corner to check it is smoking). Remove the baking tray from the grill when it begins to smoke and leave it to stand on the ground for a few minutes. Repeat this step three to four times. Remove the foil to check whether the onions and oil have taken on colour. Otherwise, repeat the procedure a few more times.

3 Place the onions in a sterilised glass jar, pour the oil over and seal the jar. If you like, you can fry the onions quickly in some oil just before serving – this will add heat to the onions and the flavours will blossom once again.

SMOKED TOMATOES

500 g (1 lb 2 oz) tomatoes

1 garlic bulb, halved widthways

fresh mixed herbs, e.g. rosemary and thyme

rind of 1 unwaxed lemon

200 ml (7 fl oz/scant 1 cup) rapeseed (canola) oil

½ teaspoon salt

100–200 g (3½–7 oz) smoker chips

1 Light the barbecue (grill). Get a large baking tray and a smaller heatproof plate with a 1–1½ cm (½ in) high edge (the edge cannot be higher than the one on the large baking tray). Place a thin layer of smoker chips in the bottom of the large baking tray then place the smaller plate in the tray.

2 Position the tomatoes, garlic, herbs and grated lemon rind on the smaller plate. Drizzle with the oil and sprinkle with the salt. Cover with kitchen foil and place the baking tray with the plate on the grill while there are still flames. After a few minutes, the chips will begin to smoke and the smoke will seep out from under the foil (if the smoke doesn't seep out, you can unfold the foil a little at one corner to check it is smoking). Remove the baking tray from the grill when it begins to smoke and leave it to stand on the ground for a few minutes. Repeat this step three to four times. Remove the foil to check whether the tomatoes and oil have taken on colour. Otherwise, repeat the procedure a few more times.

3 Place the smoked tomatoes in a sterilised glass jar, pour the oil over and seal the jar. If you like, you can fry the tomatoes quickly in some oil just before serving – this will add heat to the tomatoes and the flavours will blossom once again.

SMOKE WITHOUT FIRE **If you are unable to get hold of smoker chips or you don't have a barbecue at home, you can cheat to obtain that smoky flavour by sautéing onions or tomatoes in a frying pan with oil and a little liquid smoke.**

FERMENTED TREE ONIONS

250 g (9 oz) tree onions or any type of onion

200 ml (7 fl oz/scant 1 cup) water

10 g (2 teaspoons) salt, without iodine

2 tablespoons White Kimchi Base (optional),
    see recipe on p. 164

1 small root from a Chinese cabbage or white
    cabbage (20–30 g/¾–1 oz)

1 Remove the outermost layer from the tree onions then break off all the parts and place in a bowl.

2 Boil the water and add the salt. Stir thoroughly to ensure all the salt dissolves. Leave to cool then pour over the tree onions in the mixing bowl. Add the White Kimchi Base if you have it on hand – this is mostly acting as seasoning and you can get away without it.

3 Place the cabbage root in a 1 litre (34 fl oz/ 4 cups) sterilised clip-top preserving jar with a rubber seal (such as a Kilner jar) and add a few spoons of brine from the bowl containing the tree onions. Add the tree onions and press them down with a spoon. Pour in enough brine to cover, but leave 1–2 cm (½– ¾ in) of air at the top. Fill a plastic bag with some water, knot the bag and add it on top as a weight. Close the lid and seal.

4 Place the jar on a plate and ideally stand it in a plastic bag since it is very likely that some liquid will seep out (make sure you don't seal the bag at the top). Leave at room temperature for 4–5 days.

5 Put the jar in the refrigerator and leave for at least 2 weeks so that the flavours have time to develop – the longer you leave it, the better it will taste.

FERMENTED GARLIC **Tree onions form in certain types of onion above ground. If you don't have access to tree onions, it's fine to use garlic instead. The principle is the same.**

WHISKY-PICKLED MUSTARD SEEDS

4 teaspoons mustard seeds, preferably a mixture
    of yellow and brown

100 ml (3½ fl oz/scant ½ cup) apple cider vinegar

90 g (3½ oz/scant ½ cup) cane sugar

100 ml (3½ fl oz/scant ½ cup) water

3 tablespoons whisky

1 teaspoon salt

1 Boil the mustard seeds in lightly salted water. Reduce the heat and simmer until the seeds are completely soft, around 40– 60 minutes. Drain the liquid.

2 Boil the vinegar, sugar, water, whisky, salt and pre-boiled mustard seeds. Stir until the sugar has dissolved. Remove the saucepan from the heat and leave to cool.

3 Transfer everything to a sterilised glass jar and keep in the refrigerator.

QUICK-PICKLED BABY ONIONS

12 baby onions

1.5 litres (50 fl oz/6 cups) water

1 tablespoon salt

Syrup

100 ml (3½ fl oz/scant ½ cup) white wine vinegar

90 g (3½ oz/scant ½ cup) cane sugar

100 ml (3½ fl oz/scant ½ cup) water

2 teaspoons whole black peppercorns

2 teaspoons coriander seeds

1 Peel the onions and cut a cross into the top of each one. Boil the water and salt and add the onions. Boil for 8–10 minutes. Drain the onions and rinse until cold. Set aside.

2 Mix the vinegar, sugar, water, black peppercorns and coriander seeds in a saucepan and put on a medium heat. Bring to the boil and stir for around 2 minutes until the sugar has dissolved completely.

3 Put the onions in a sterilised glass jar and pour the hot syrup over them. Leave to cool and then cover with the lid. Leave to stand in the refrigerator for at least 1 hour.

PICKLED WILD GARLIC CAPERS

1 kg (2 lb 4 oz) wild garlic capers

650 g (1 lb 7 oz/generous 2 cups) salt

300–400 ml (10–13 fl oz/1¼–generous 1½ cups)
   Champagne vinegar or white wine vinegar

1 Cut the capers off the fruiting head as best as possible to make it easier to use them when they are ready. Place the capers and salt in a glass jar and stir to ensure they are thoroughly mixed. Seal the jar and leave in a cool, dark place for at least 4 weeks.

2 Strain the capers and rinse the salt away using cold water. Take care to ensure you remove almost all the salt – the capers are already salty.

3 Put the wild garlic capers in a sterilised glass jar and fill with vinegar so that the capers are completely covered. Leave in the refrigerator for 1 week before using them.

INDEX